STUCK ON YOU

A year in the life of a Chelsea Supporter

WALTER OTTON

Stuck on You

ISBN: 978-1514733554
First published by Gate 17 2015

Cover design: Gate 17
www.gate17.co.uk

Stuck On You

is sponsored by

www.rivalsfootball.net

"More than just a football message board!"

"If this book is anything like the mess Walter was in at Southampton away in 2013, then it's not worth the paper it's written on."

WOGFTB

"If you only buy one book from a luminous orange Chelsea shorts wearing author this year, this has to be near the top of the list."

Famous

"The perfect book for when you're on the toilet…
.... and have run out of toilet roll!"

orseshit_n_amburgers

"Walter's literary career – Brown Bread."

MHLPisshead

"A damning indictment on middle aged life in the 21st century."

The_Drogs_Bollox

"So forensic in its detail CRIMINOLOGISTS love it."

Avinaliedown

"Does for literature what Enoch Powell did for race relations."

cfcww

"What a load of old flannel."

1WB

Stuck On You

A YEAR IN THE LIFE OF A CHELSEA SUPPORTER

May 2014 – May 2015

CONTENTS

AUTHOR'S NOTE

Back in 1990, the Directors at Brighton and Hove Albion FC sued the *Gull's Eye* fanzine for libel. It was around this time that I tentatively sent my first article into *The Chelsea Independent* fanzine. I remember someone telling me to create a pseudonym – that way Ken Bates would never be able to take me to court if he didn't like what I had written. And so Walter (my Grandad's name) and Otton (my Granny's maiden name) was born. So when it came to the football, the name Walter stuck.

Every month I write an article for the *cfcuk* fanzine. I always make sure I meet the deadlines. As the years have gone by, (I think I have only missed two deadlines since 2002-ish and that was when my kids were born in 2007 and 2008), it slowly dawned on me that fellow supporters actually *liked* some of the articles I'd churned out. I met people in pubs and on concourses who would shake my hand and tell me so. I cannot tell you how incredible it feels when someone I've never met before introduces themselves with an encouraging word or two regarding something I have written.

I am just a regular guy, married with two kids, who goes when he can to Chelsea when time and finances allow. When I do go, I inevitably write an article. I decided in the summer of 2014 that I would collate all the articles I end up writing to produce a *'year in the life of'* type book. These articles have featured in *cfcuk*, the *Chelsea FanCast* website and the *Plains of Almeria* website. With *Stuck on You* I am not restricted to a word count, so I have added several more paragraphs to these pieces that wouldn't have been in the original work. Plus, I have included a few articles that have never been published before – aren't you lucky!

None of this would be possible without **Mark Worrall** (GATE 17) and **David Johnstone**, plus other *cfcuk* scribes **Tim Rolls, Kelvin Barker** and **David Chidgey** who have always encouraged me along the way. I would like to thank my sponsor **Shed69** at www.rivalsfootball.net – *"More than just a football message board!"*

I would like to send a heart felt *thank you* to Jeff, the owner of The Finborough Arms, for writing the foreword. One of the happiest times of my life is when I am with my mates pre-match in a boozer. When I am not there, I crave it. When I am there, I cherish it.

I would also like to thank Callum for writing the introduction. I love the whole *spirit of the streets* that surrounds the sticker phenomena, and Cal articulates this so much better than me, which is why I am grateful for his contribution. There are a few sticker accounts out there now, however Cal and his pals birthed the original idea and to be blunt, theirs are the best.

My primary plan was to have a photo section in this book featuring the best pictures sent to me of stickers stuck in brilliant places and in splendid locations. Sadly I am not able to do this due to the Club owning the copyright to the crests. Without going into too much detail, neither GATE17 nor I are in a position to start a fight we'll never win. If the Club bans supporters and suspends memberships and season tickets for standing up at the Bridge, using a rude word on a concourse, or selling a face value ticket on to a mate, then it's probably for the best that I don't poke a lump of celery at their wasps nest by using their copyrighted crests.

I would like to dedicate this book to all the people who have sorted me out with match-tickets this season. Thanks to:

Sausage Rolls; Wee Willie Winston; Kenny Christmas; Stock Check Dave; Big Beard Bri; Bacon Roll Campo and Marathon Stan.

Finally, if your name features in these pages, then thank you for being part of my journey.
Especially **Big Chris** and **Smiffy**. You make it what it is.

You will have your own personal journey with mates and matches you have attended this season. You will have your own circle of friends, own routines and own experiences. It ended up, of course, being a very special season indeed – beating Tottenham at Wembley to win the League Cup and winning the Football League for the first time since 2010. So, here is my personal journey, being stuck on Chelsea, as it happened.

@WalterOtton
JULY 2015

FOREWORD

By Jeff Bell
Landlord of the Finborough Arms

People who are not followers of football often find the dedication of those that are, strange. When they hear someone say that football is their life, they find it stranger still, even worrying.

Our national sport was always in the background of my own life. I was a supporter of non-league South Shields as a teenager, but never a fan of a top-flight club. When I became landlord of the empty Finborough Arms, that changed. I knew the pub had once been a favourite of the Chelsea fans, so I sought to revive the tradition. I am now lucky enough to count dozens of loyal Chelsea fans as my friends. What I've learned from them is that football is, indeed, life.

The more successful a club is, the more expensive and time-consuming it is to follow. Away fixtures are no longer just national, but sometimes international. True, the glory might be more frequent, but football comes at an ever greater cost. Of course the games of top-flight clubs are frequently televised, so it's possible to be an armchair fan. This makes the dedication of the dedicated Chelsea fans I have met all the more remarkable.

The relationships formed between fans cross all divides (other than that of football itself, of course). Instead of only meeting people of a usually similar background through the humdrum of everyday existence, people are bound together by one shared passion with often very little else in common. It is that shared passion that gives an intensity to their comradeship. They might only meet weekly or fortnightly in the football season, and over summer not at all, but the bond is stronger for it.

Why is football life? Because it punctuates it. A year in the life of a football fan has all the same sadnesses and joys as everyone else's: the same triumphs to savour and adversity to overcome. But all the while there is the fixture list to consider, the next warm-up in the pub, the thrill of taking your place and joining in the cheer. Win or lose, the football puts the rest of the fan's life in perspective.

STUCK ON YOU

Introduction by Callum West

The Original Chelsea Stickers

I think the biggest influence on the stickers at Chelsea has been going away in Europe.

As much as experience of a new city and the piss up on European away trips, I have always been intrigued by the varying local football cultures across Europe – and stickers are a big thing across the continent. I'm a prolific pub toilet vandal, always carving CHELSEA or CFC into doors with my keys or daubing them haphazardly on the tiles if I had a pen to hand. However, in the pub toilets across Europe, they were filed not just with this style of amateur football graffiti but football stickers, piled on top of one another or half peeled off by an angry rival.

For me as a kid, football stickers were Frank Sinclair and John Spencer in Merlin books, (all got, got need), but across the continent they had long been used by ultras as a display of *'Galatasaray* (or whoever) *Were* Here', it was about fans leaving their mark. Whether they be travelling with their side, or had just happened to find themselves at a train station, in the pub, or by a particular lamppost – the circumstance meant there was an opportunity to leave a stamp on their location.

Living in a cosmopolitan part of West London these were also popping up at home, suddenly the road sign at the end of my street was seemingly the battleground for a sticker war taking place between ultras following third division Polish sides. These were typically European Ultra in the design – pyro and muscular cartoon fans with scarves round their faces. Presumably declaring that this side had fans that were harder, more loyal and better at setting off fireworks than their rivals. However, save for the odd United *'Viva Ken Barlow'*, it was almost entirely the preserve of continental sides.

The first time it struck me that we could and should do these ourselves was before the QPR cup game in 2012. There had been a bit of needle between the clubs and specifically the fans following their victory in the league game earlier that season. And as lads who live not far from Loftus Road, and who grew up with a lot of mates who supported QPR, it seemed like a laugh and a wind up in equal measure for me and a pal to go over Shepherds Bush the night before and stick Chelsea crests and 'Pride of London' stickers in as many places as possible. Looking back the quality of these was awful – scaled badly and printed on the address labels you get at work – but it was a bit of a buzz doing it and it got a bit of a rise out of QPR supporting mates.

Following winning in Munich, a few other lads keen to inform our rivals at any opportunity that we had won the European Cup, had got some made for themselves of varying aesthetic quality, and you'd see them crop up from time to time. Under my bed I still had a few left over after the evening prior to QPR, so I would use these to ping up in away ground toilets and on European trips now and then.

English football fans aghast at the decimation of our football culture have been looking towards the continent for inspiration in recent years, and whilst some, like Palace, have gone the whole hog and declared themselves ultras, I think most are keen to put their own spin on it. That was certainly the case for the people I go to football with, we've no desire to dress in black and sing songs with no words in all game, but the colour and passion of the ultras we had seen on trips following Chelsea in Europe had definitely rubbed off. The English terraces had a reputation for humour that marks them out as different from their European counterparts and I think that's where the *'Ruining Football'* thing came from. It's firmly tongue in cheek and it's a wind up. I had the idea for it as a flag and considering my complete lack of IT skills, I asked a pal to design it when it struck me that it would be perfect for a sticker, and it snowballed from there. Another pal set up a website to sell them and also chucked in the odd design idea, as well as loads of other lads getting in on the act.

I think some of the designs you see now miss the point a bit and I'm always disappointed in anything that uses the contemporary badge rather than the Earl of Cadogan coat of arms badge. However, the sheer variety of stickers now (after what started as a niche thing) is well impressive, and I saw a beautiful Peter Osgood one in a pub at St Pancras before Arsenal a few weeks back.

I am also proud that it's one of the developments in football fan culture in England that Chelsea can genuinely say that we are at the forefront of.

Hopefully there'll be a few good ones next year to celebrate this title.

@CFCCallum

http://cfcstickers.bigcartel.com/category/chelsea

@cfcstickers

THANK YOU VERY MUCH FOR FRANKIE LAMPARD

"I don't actually think there is a way to translate into words what Lampard has meant to the club and fans." @cfc_jb

Indeed. What can you say about Frank Lampard? On May 23rd 2014, Chelsea Football Club published a list of players who they were releasing, because their contracts were terminating on the 01st of June. Both Ashley Cole and Frank James Lampard were on that list. Suffice to say, a lot of hearts skipped a beat. Frank had been at Chelsea for 13 years. That is 33% of my life. THIRTY THREE PERCENT. If you take into account Frank's 211 goals for Chelsea that means (a friend of mine more intelligent than me worked this out) that Frank has scored a goal for Chelsea every two months I've been alive. Or, if you work out what his 211 goals over 13 years means – Frank scored a goal for Chelsea every 1.62 days of our lives over that 13 year period.

Here's how it was worked out:

13 years x 12 months = 156 months at Chelsea FC.

Remove the months of June and July:

13 years x 10 months = 130 months actively playing for Chelsea FC.

Divide his 211 goals by the 130 months, and a goal was scored every 1.62307692307 of a day, by Frank, for me, for you and for Chelsea Football Club.

Now, I know you could be pedantic about it and point out he might score four in one game, then have a 'dry' spell – just humour me for a bit regarding this – that on average, when you break it down like that, Frank's goals are embedded over a huge chunk of both my life and yours.

A typical twenty-one-year old supporter, for example, would have been nine years old when Frank signed. They were in Year 5, taken exams in Year 6, gone up to Secondary School, studied through Years 7, 8, 9, 10 and 11, taken their GCSEs, their first cigarette, their first drink, gone to college for two years, had an eighteenth birthday party, got a job or left the family home to go to University, lost their virginity, maybe had a child of their own, possibly got a degree or been working for a few years and celebrated each time that Frank scored one of his 211 goals.

We are all on an alternative, unique journey. My path through life is different to yours. It is fascinating to think that our experiences, memories and 'life-markers' somewhere along the line tie-in to and relate to, various goals Frank has scored. Here are a handful of a few of mine:

Frank Lampard Senior broke Everton hearts:
Toffee Colin returns from relieving his bladder, walks towards me at the bar and pulls up a stool. I tell him I'm writing an article about Super Frank and he tells me about an FA Cup Semi Final replay in 1980 between Everton and West Ham at Elland Road. Colin gulps his drink down then smiles, folds his arms and paints a picture for me of the terracing, the ground and the pitch – well over thirty years ago but he recalls it clearly – he tells me he reckons 4000 West Ham were there (after seeing the footage I reckon it could be 7000) and the rest of Elland Road was full of Everton. A 0-0 draw meant extra time and Alan Devonshire (Ed De Goey look a like) put the

Hammers in front – Toffee Colin becomes animated as he describes Bob Latchford's equaliser – he stands up and recreates Latchford jumping on the fence as the Everton end well and truly fell. Then Colin goes on to describe how time stood still shortly before the full time whistle as a diving header by Frank Lampard Senior squeezed past Martin Hodge in the Everton goal. It provided a heart-breaking split-second moment of silence for him and the thousands of other Toffees before the roar kicks in from all the Irons fans in the ground as they realise the ball is in the net. I do a quick Google search to see when Frank Junior was born. He was only 18 months old when this match took place, when his Dads winning goal took West Ham to Wembley.

It wasn't until I looked at the YouTube footage of this game that I realised it was the game when Frank Lampard Senior did his famous impromptu jig around the corner flag after his winning goal.

When Chelsea signed Frank Lampard Junior in 2001 it was a lot of money at the time. Many eyebrows were raised. As Toffee Colin meanders over to the other side of the bar to serve a thirsty customer, I sink half of my fresh pint of London Pride in one hit and begin making a few notes…

St Mary's, Southampton, Wednesday 28th August 2002:

It was the summer of 2002. I was leaving South London to take a job down on the South Coast. It was a huge time of transition for me. I had not renewed my season ticket. I was moving home and starting a new job after twenty-seven years living and working within the same four-mile radius. There was a lot of stress going on. The new season began and Smiffy drove us in the work minibus to Southampton away and we parked in the Toys R Us car park. It was a Wednesday night. The game was a 1-1 draw. Due to the events in my life at the time, I needed my Chelsea medicine. Sometimes you long for a goal to go in so you can have that release; Let out that roar; Have that celebration; Embrace that liberation. The Saints went one up. Trouble was brewing in our end with the taunts from the opposition supporters. A Chelsea fan jumped over the netting that covered the seats to get to the Saints fans. He was arrested and marched in front the Chelsea fans to chants of support. I recall a certain Jimmy Floyd Hasselbaink that night. All week reports in the media were that Barca were tabling a bid for him. He strolled through the game – actually strolling is an exaggeration – he dawdled through the match showing no interest whatsoever for Chelsea FC despite his vast wages and the hard earned money the supporters had coughed up travelling to see him play for the team we love. So, from that moment on I always looked at JFH a little differently. Then Super Frank equalised. There was the release; the celebration; the liberation I craved. The 'Super Frank' chant went up. Smiffy and I walked back to the minibus and the Toys R Us gates were locked. I had to lean with all my weight against a bush, pushing it back, while Smiffy drove over the kerb and between two bushes to get out the car park.

Reebok Stadium, Bolton, Saturday 30th April 2005:

The Doris and I were in Australia for three months. When Jose became our manager in the summer of 2004 I certainly didn't think we'd win the league – I thought maybe the season after. A true Chelsea pessimistic! So we booked some time away travelling. I had spent three days on a boat cruising around the Whitsunday Islands and on return to the mainland I couldn't get hold of a newspaper! My friend Blanco drove for several hours to Rockhampton and on the way we stopped at a petrol station. I flicked to the sports pages of a paper to find a small section saying: *"Chelsea win the English Premier League: Joe Cole danced on the roof of the Chelsea team coach as hundreds of fans surrounded the vehicle in the car park celebrating after Frank Lampards goals confirmed Chelsea as League Champions."* I was there in spirit. Thank you, Super Frank.

Stamford Bridge, Wednesday 30th April 2008: Champions League Penalty against Liverpool:

This was perhaps the turning point in the media's manipulation of Frank (they had a change of heart) and also (maybe as a result) the public's general perception of Frank as a man, a son and a father as well as a footballer. His mother, Pat, had passed away six days earlier. He took a penalty. In extra-time. He scored the penalty. After the out-pouring of emotion, Drogba had to put his arms around Frank's body and drag him up. The last time I saw Chelsea fans in tears at the Bridge was before we played Spurs after Matthew Harding had died. What a man. Martin Samuels article after this match was one of the most poignant pieces of journalism I have ever read. A year later Frank rang into a radio show to protest about some untrue media reports about his private life. It wasn't like he had to do anything further to go up in our estimations of respect and support – nevertheless this was still the outcome. Rest in Peace, Pat Lampard.

Wembley, FA Cup Final v Everton, Saturday 30th May 2009:

The Frank Lampard Senior goal versus Everton I mentioned earlier went down in West Ham history. Hammers fans had a song about it:

"I'm dreaming of a Frank Lampard. Just like the one at Elland Road. When the ball came over, and Frank fell over, and scored the fucking winning goal."

In the first half, Drogba equalised Saha's early strike. In the second half Frank scored the winning goal. Off he trotted to the corner flag, copying his Dads celebration by doing a jig around the corner flag. Twenty-nine years separated the two goals against Everton – and poor Toffee Colin can remember both of them like they were yesterday.

Anfield, Liverpool, Sunday 02nd May 2010:
As the home crowd sang YNWA pre-match, the *CHELSEA CHELSEA CHELSEA* from the away end was the most defiant I have ever heard it. We simply had to win up here to go into our final game of the season at home against Wigan – beat Liverpool and beat Wigan and we win the league. At times I couldn't join in the chant, I was literally choked up with anxiety and anticipation. On 33 minutes, Stevie G made a dreadful back pass and Drogba scored in front of the Kop. We were denied a clear penalty when Kalou was fouled by Lucas. In the 54th minute Anelka beat the offside trap and squared the ball for Frank to finish. If I were to study my legs closely I reckon I can still find some bruises on them sustained from the carnage that followed. As the match moved into its dying minutes the Chelsea hordes sang *"We're*

gonna win the league" over and over and over and over again. Frank had sealed our win. We were then treated with Rafa Benitez and his squad doing a lap of 'honour' at full time where he and his Captain, along with Carragher, were serenaded to some most wonderful chants from the travelling support. The loss for Liverpool also meant they couldn't qualify for the Champions League. It doesn't get much better than that. Taxi Alan and I smiled all the way home. I think Champagne Les is still grinning. *"You're ancient history"* we sang. I could die a happy man. Frank – you're becoming a living legend to us.

Barcelona, Monday 23rd April 2012:

It was the night before the semi-final second leg of the European Cup. Smiffy and I were in Las Rambla chatting to a bird with false eye lashes who was inviting us to her restaurant (we later obliged) when the sound of *Chelsea Chelsea Chelsea* carried on the breeze, wrapped its hand around us and drew us into Cheers bar for a proper session with a load of Chels. As the songs went on and the bar filled up, a West Ham fan appeared from the other side of the bar (he'd been there longer than Smiffy and I eating his meal with friends at the rear of the establishment) and he obviously couldn't stand the songs any longer and duly (and bravely) stood and started singing *Bubbles.* As you can imagine, he got verbally annihilated – all in good spirits: *The wheels on your house go round and round; You love your caravan; ...and like West Ham they fade and die; Avram Grant took you down la la la la la; Gianfranco Zola;* the list goes on. The best song was saved until last. We danced with delight as San Miguel spilt from our glasses and generous servings of rum and coke swilling with the ice splashed out of our goblets as we sang to the lone Hammer:

Thank you very much for Frankie Lampard – thank you very much thank you very very very much! Thank you very much for Frankie Lampard – thank you very very very very very very very very very very very MUCH!

Of all the photos of Frank taken during his Chelsea career, my favourite is the picture taken after Torres scored in the Nou Camp. Fernando's team-mates are steaming over to surround him, Frank is the first there. We've only gone and done them in their own back-yard to reach Munich. With ten men. And Bosingwa at centre-back. And a Messi missed penalty. Frank has sunk down on one knee with a huge smile on his boat, the Captain's armband proudly over his left bicep – and he is looking up at five thousand of us in the top tier going absolutely fucking mental.

So, Frank.... If I ever bump into you, and should I muster the courage to step up, I'm sure, to you, I'll be just another fan wanting a chat – but to me you've been, week in, week out, a massive part of my life. Cheers for everything, Frank.

DAVID LUIZ MOREIRA MARINHO

"Both cultured and kamikaze."

#Geezer

You know how it went. PSG whacked in an substantial offer for Sideshow Bob and it was accepted. The deal went through on June 13th 2014 and I duly wrote this piece for Stamford Chidge and the *Chelsea FanCast* website.

Some say there is no room for sentiment in football. However, I'm the kind of bloke that finds it impossible to detach sentiment and emotion from the game. Sure, players come and go. I know all too well the adage that gets dragged out intermittently – pointing to the fact that us fans will always be there whereas owners, managers, fitness coaches, tea-ladies and players will all come and go. But we stay. The hole that Juan Mata left in some supporters' hearts is still gaping today. Pour scorn on that if you will, but it won't change how some Chelsea feel. So, as far as it goes for me and my emotional attachments – I truly am a sentimental supporter.

When I was a young person, like many young people do, I cherry picked Chelsea games according to the cash in my wallet. I had a paper round on Thursdays after school and I also worked a part-time Saturday job in a warehouse and when the summer holidays hit I spent a lot of it working to save up. I loved standing on the Shed, especially when it was rammed, craning for a view of the action as the crowd surged and swayed, groaned in despair or roared and rejoiced.

When I turned 21, my parents bought me a season ticket for my birthday. It cost £421. It was in the West Stand just above the benches. Ruud Gullit was my favourite player. He could play anywhere along the back, anywhere in mid-field or up front. I watched him slot in, as and when, to those positions. Gullit has often stated in interviews that it was at Chelsea that he enjoyed his career the most and felt the happiest. He ended his first season by being named runner-up to Eric Cantona as Footballer of the Year.

As a fan, Ruudi put a smile on my face or gave me an in-take of breath or made me shake my head in awe at a pass or a piece of skill – in some ways his signing encapsulated the 'new' Chelsea which developed as the years went by – British players mixing in with the foreign signings. When Gullit led Chelsea out at Wembley in May 1997 this was clear to see. Our squad included: Frank Sinclair and Frank LeBoeuf; Scott Minto and Dan Petrescu; Dennis Wise and Bobby Di Matteo; Mark Hughes and Gianfranco Zola; the subs bench including Andy Myers and Gianluca Vialli.

We've all got our favourite players, for whatever reasons, whether they be past or present. David Luiz is, for me, exactly that. Maybe it's because (I'm a Londoner) of certain similarities he shares with Ruudi. Maybe, when I watched Luiz play, it subconsciously took me back to a time in my youth when Chelsea were evolving and on the up – starting with Glenn Hoddle taking over Chelsea and the team qualifying for Europe in 1994/95 after United completed the double and we were runners-up in the FA Cup. Why would it do that – I mean, why would Ruud Gullit remind me of David Luiz? Maybe it was the hair? Maybe it was the number 4 shirt?

Or maybe it was his style and his pure ability. I mean, he could nip in and nick a ball, couldn't he? Timing and precision. Or pick a pass with either foot. Or playing quick one / two's and pinging a ball to a team-mate that no-one in the stadium saw was on. He was comfortable at right back. Or left back. And, if it was to be adopted – he had the capability play in the sweeper system. Oh – and he could play in either Centre-back position. What about the holding midfield role? Job done. Right of midfield? Yep. Left of midfield? That too. Take a free-kick? You bet. Belt one in from thirty yards? That, and some. Up front? Yeah – if desperate times called for desperate measures.

Mark Lawrenson hated David Luiz. In the Confederations Cup in 2013, Luiz went right through Cavani (I think) in the first few minutes of Brazil v Uruguay and rightly got booked. It was both rash but purposeful. Have it. Jonathan Pearce said: "Lawro – what has David Luiz got to learn about defending?" Lawro answered: "Everything."

The pundits and experts tore a strip of him whenever they could. Sometimes Chelsea fans did too. But make no mistake – Luiz has the medals to prove otherwise. He went off injured in the FA Cup semi-final when Chelsea smashed Tottenham 5-1. He missed the FA Cup final and the Barca game in the Nou Camp with the injury. But he made Munich. Some say he and Cahill were only 70 or 80% fit. Ah,

Munich. Sweet, glorious Munich...

....What about his run-up for his penalty, eh? Luiz is a mad-man. A maverick. He's bloody mental. Mata had missed his pen. So Luiz HAD to score. And he goes and takes a run-up like that. This is the EUROPEAN CUP FINAL, MAN. Not Sensible bloody Soccer on the Amiga 500. I bet that you, the reader, were shitting yourself when Luiz began that ridiculous run-up, yeah? Bet you're smiling reading this now though, aren't you? And after Luiz buried it he then gave it to the Bayern fans behind the goal. Oh yes.

Oh David Luiz – you are the love of my life.

Sideshow Bob signed for Chelsea on 30/01/2011. He made his debut on February 6th replacing Bosingwa (in the rain, Bosingwa in the rain) in a 1-0 home loss to the Bin Dippers. On a Monday night in February – Valentines Day in fact – Luiz made his first start for Chelsea in a 0-0 draw with Fulham.

The subsequent edition of *cfcuk* in March 2011, had one of the best front covers of all time: **Eleven David Luiz's.** When he arrived at Chelsea it was like a bomb had gone off. Sure, it petered out. I get that. Anyhow, here is an adapted version of the article I had printed in that edition from sentimental old me.

I'm gonna miss you, Geez.

Fulham 0-0 Chelsea
Monday 14th February 2011

I step out the carriage at Worcester Park and jog down the steps, prepared to pop into the florist on the left hand side. I pause for a bit, doing a double-take because a younger bloke and a girl are working – and I was expecting the old boy with snow white hair to be serving the customers like me that have bounced off the train. I can picture him now. I walked past him day after day and year after year on my way to and from work.... maybe he retired, anyway, I choose a bunch of flowers and continue up the High Street to my sister's place.

I realise I'm observing the familiar shops on the walk up: Super Fish; Iceland; Ross the Fruiterer; KFC; The Halifax; Pizza Express; Rumours and two charity shops. I reach my destination and ring the bell, my sisters friend answers the door and lets me in because my sister can't make it to the door. She is heavily pregnant with a C section booked in for seven days time. I didn't tell her I was coming because she would've told me not to, so I guess it's a nice surprise for her. I lay the flowers on the table and stay for a few minutes. I'm sitting next to her on the sofa – suddenly she grabs my hand and rests it on her tummy to one side. I can feel the baby kicking – my nephew – seven days until he enters the world and Chelsea will have a new supporter – and I stay there for about a minute and I start to well up – I know it's time to go before I start to get too emotional, so I squeeze her hand and make a move. I walk up Cheam Common Road past the church and a few others shops – a curry house and a glazers – then offices and bus stops before I hit North Cheam and stroll into Wetherspoons and there he is – Millsy the Surrey Scouser propping up the bar with a Stella in his hand and a daft grin on his face. I haven't seen him for a year – it's been that long since I was last boozing down this neck of the woods.

I grab a Corona and we move to the seats for a sit down and a proper catch up. I watch the bubbles fizz at the lime and drink long and drink deep – Millsy and I pick up right where we left off – a sign of a good friendship, that.

After a couple more drinks I leave the pub and jump on a 93 bus. It starts in North Cheam and goes all the way to Putney Bridge – and for some reason I jog up the stairs to the top deck and sit right at the front of the bus as if I were a kid on my way to my way to Kingston with my Mum on the 65 bus (which was later renamed the 71 – same route, different number) and I look out the window for most of the journey taking it all in – Morden, Wimbledon Common,

Putney Heath and then finally Putney Bridge. This is South West London.

I jump off before the bus goes over the Bridge and I take in the Thames. It's a cold night but still and refreshing. I wonder down to the Half Moon where Taxi Alan, Smiffy and Den await. We have a drink then move on to the curry house. I pick at my food, realising my appetite has gone. I find myself worrying about my sister and my nephew – the alcohol heightening my concerns regarding the impending C section. I reflect on the few minutes I had at her house. She's melted into the sofa, her head back, cheeks puffed out, staring at the ceiling. She makes a painful face then takes my hand, placing it on her swelled belly. I feel my nephew kicking for England in her womb. Mental. I laugh at the wonder of it all. Smiffy snaps his fingers which breaks me out of my zone. He's asking me if I'm going to finish my food. I shake my head, he reaches over and takes my plate – I turn to the waiter and ask for another drink, asking the others if they want another one too. They all do. The waiter prepares more drinks as Smiffy demolishes my curry.

We leave a generous tip and make for Craven Cottage. Strolling through Bishops Park with the Thames to our left I notice a mist settling over the water. The away support are buoyed with the news that David Luiz and Fernando Torres are starting the match. Some people in front of me are chatting about Valentines Day – I had completely forgotten about it. My day began getting up early – my kids and wife still asleep – I grabbed a bag from under the bed that I'd been hiding and went downstairs – arranging their presents on the kitchen table: A blue matchbox car for my boy (aged 2), a tin of sweets for my girl (just turned 4) and half a dozen red roses for the Doris. Except, that when I laid the roses out I counted only four roses instead of the six that there should have been. But that was this morning. And this is now. Chelsea away. My other love.

I was buzzing after Luiz's full debut. He was everywhere. Okay, he gave the penalty away, but his versatility, passion, vision and drive is there for all to see. Even if Cech let him massively off the hook to earn a draw, Chelsea deserved the three points. Our supporters were in great voice:

Bounce in a Minute; We don't hate You, You're just Shit; Double Double Double; One Man Went to Mow! My favourite chant *Chelsea / Champions* resounded around the Cottage and drifted over the Thames.

I grabbed a lift back to the South Coast from a Fulham supporting mate of mine who lives in my area. I returned home just after midnight. I wearily climbed the stairs and went into my kids' bedroom to find them, as expected, fast asleep in their bunk-beds. I kissed my sleeping daughter first and then my son. His duvet was half off the bed. I tucked him in and noticed he had his new Blue toy car by his pillow. I kissed his head and smiled because his Mum had dressed him in his favourite Chelsea pyjamas.

I crawl into bed and but my head on the pillow staring at the ceiling. I run through moments of the match in my head. David Luiz. Brazilian flair. He's going to be great for us.

Other significant moments in David Luiz's Chelsea career:
After his first start for Chelsea in a 0-0 draw with Fulham, he was awarded Man of the Match despite giving away a 93rd minute penalty which Petr Cech saved. The BBC website said: *"Luiz had been a phenomenal performer for the visitors."*

On 14/03/2012 in the Champions League, his stunning performance at Stamford Bridge earned him UEFA *Man of the Match* in the 4-1 extra time win versus Napoli.

Luiz was awarded *Man of the Match* in the 8-0 thrashing of Villa on 23/12/2012. He scores a quality free-kick.

There was a trend of grown men buying (and loving the fact they were wearing) David Luiz wigs. One supporter up at Blackpool on a Monday night (thanks SKY you cunts) wears a wig as he takes part in a half-time fan competition.

Away to WBA on 16/11 (Chelsea won 3-1) I witnessed two Chelsea fans in the queue for pre-match beers start kicking off with each other. No-one could take the row seriously as one of the blokes had a David Luiz wig on. The stewards threw them both out and everyone was laughing.

On a beautiful, warm Wednesday evening, David Luiz's incredible strike opened the scoring at Craven Cottage on 17/04/2013. The Chelsea support sang for the entire match including, in the second half, a thirteen minute rendition of *"We are the Champions! Champions of Europe!"* I know it was thirteen minutes long, because I timed it. The chant resounded across the Thames, and with the supporters stomping their feet on the wooden floors, we made a proper racket.

I took a coach from The Wee Imp to Basel for the UEFA Cup Semi-Final first leg on 25/04/2013. In fairness, Chelsea were crap. Luiz's last minute free-kick wins the game. We all go mad and leave the ground singing: *"Amsterdam, Amsterdam, we are coming!"*

The journey was made both bearable and memorable because of the company – including No Beans Kenny, Tape-Mix Tim the Squadron Leader and Sausage Rolls.

The photo of Luiz laying hands on Fernando Torres head and praying for him became rather iconic for those followers of Jesus. However, not even the Good Lord could sort out Fernando's lack of pace and control, though after the Nou Camp and Amsterdam no-one really gives a hoot about anything else.

Farewell video by @feroze17
https://www.youtube.com/watch?v=0EQahuuT53U&list=UUc8RKUy9YnvfvdIGpwDvB6A

Finally, here is another perspective on this website regarding Luiz by Ross Mooring. Includes the quite brilliant apt phrase: "both cultured and kamikaze." That he was, that he is, and that he shall always be. Both cultured and kamikaze.
http://chelseafancast.com/2014/05/season-in-review-david-luiz/

AFC WIMBLEDON V CHELSEA

A Chelsea supporter's perspective

The editor of the Wimbledon match day programme contacted the *Chelsea Supporters Trust* and asked if they would like to make a contribution to the programme ahead of our teams meeting in a friendly at Kingsmeadow on 19th July. The CST asked if I would consider writing a piece. I jumped at the opportunity to make my début writing for an official programme. (The editor considered would be for the best to omit the section where I have a dig at Peter Winkelman and the MK Dons franchise, which is completely understandable.) For those of you who couldn't make the match or didn't buy a programme, Stamford Chidge put the article on the *Chelsea FanCast* website. My thanks goes out to him, the @ChelseaSTrust and also to Ray Armfield / @KentWomble at AFC Wimbledon for including my article:

When the clubs announced that this pre-season friendly was taking place, a whole variety of thoughts and memories personal to me are conjured for several reasons regarding the fixture, the venue and our grounds.

Chelsea fans of a certain vintage will remember the annual summer fixture playing Kingstonian. It was local, it was cheap, and if you weren't on your summer holidays you'd arrange to go with your mates who you might not have seen for a month or so since the back-end of the previous season.

I recall a match at the Bridge in October 1996. Frank LeBouef clashed heads with Robbie Earle and played the rest of the match with a large egg shaped lump on his head, covered by a ridiculous bandage. The Wombles won 4-2 with goals coming from Earle, Ardley, Gayle and Ekoku. Chelsea's scorers were Minto and Vialli. The victory gave Wimbledon a club record seven wins in a row. We met again six months later in the FA Cup semi final at Highbury. Wimbledon had the Clock End and most the West Stand, Chelsea the Northbank and everywhere else. I was in the East Stand and had a quite beautiful view of Zola's incredible goal as Chelsea won 3-0 to book their place at Wembley.

Vinnie Jones played for both clubs. He left Wimbledon to sign for Leeds, Sheffield United, Chelsea then back to Wimbledon in the early stages of the 92-93 season. At Stamford Bridge during the pre-match warm-ups, the Shed end used to chant, *"Vinnie, Vinnie gis' a song"* – he would jog over, cup his hands over his mouth and yell, *"One Man Went to Mow!"*, then proceed to conduct the supporters as we sang the song. After Vinnie left Chelsea to re-join Wimbledon, I went to Selhurst Park in December 1992 as a crowd of 14,687 saw a dreadful 0-0 draw. The highlight of the day was when the away fans chanted for Vinnie to once more *"gis' a song"* and he jogged over, unzipped his tracksuit top to reveal a Chelsea top (which we all cheered) and, for the last time, he conducting us as we belted out the chant.

Chelsea fans know what it is like to nearly lose our ground. *"Cash For Chelsea"* buckets were on the forecourt in 1977 and *"Save The Bridge"* buckets in 1982. More recently in 2011, the CPO (Chelsea Pitch Owners) which consists of thousands of Chelsea supporters who have purchased a share, have had to stand, vote and fight against the Clubs hierarchy who tried to buy back the free-hold owned by CPO in order to force a move away from Stamford Bridge. It is a boiling pot of politics and emotion, of supporters versus the Board, which is always simmering behind the backdrop of our recent on-pitch successes.

I, along with hundreds of thousands of other supporters, watched with horror as weasel-faced Winkelman gave birth to his odious football franchise. Personally, I wish AFC Wimbledon would smash the MK Dons 10-0 at every given opportunity and hopefully one day Winkelman's club will ultimately embrace liquidation.

So, don't be fooled that Chelsea fans are classless, or a bunch of plastics. Of course we are grateful to Mr Abramovich for all he has done for our Club. But make no mistake, we would travel in our thousands whether we were playing Barnsley or Barcelona. We are more than happy that this summer our team aren't touring Malaysia or Thailand! We can follow our team once again back at good old Kingsmeadow and genuinely wish AFC Wimbledon all the best this season on the pitch and also in their pursuit for a future stadium that they can finally, since Plough Lane, call home.

AWAY GAMES SEASON PREVIEW 2014/15

Trainers, Betting, Away Games and Chelsea

Young whippersnapper @JTweedsPOA is an analytical master. Whenever I read his articles after matches, he highlights aspects of the game tactically and succinctly that I was completely ignorant of, to be honest. Joe, and his website comrades both at 'Plains of Almeria' and 'WAGNH', compiled a breathtakingly intricate preview of the 2014/15 season. It was available as a free download before the season kicked off, along with the option of donating to the *'Help a London Child'* charity. After a week or so, over 5000 downloads were made and over £1200 donated. I was delighted to contribute, here is my piece:

Hello! And welcome to my preview of season 2014/15. If you want to read about **formations, tactics, vortexes, reverse triangles and double pivots** then stop now! **I'll leave that to the experts!** Trust me, I learn a lot from them (mostly stuff that passes me by during a match), and it takes all sorts, coz I'm more about the bets and the booze. And decent trainers.

August 2014:

Right, first things, first – you've got to get your new season clobber sorted. You also get a **severe ticking off** if you fail to have purchased a **cfcuk** fanzine and have it rolled up and shoved in your back right jeans pocket. When it comes to trainers, personally, I'm a **New Balance** man and I have been since 2010 after I read an article on how they are Top of the Pops in terms of **ethics** and that, and **Nike** are the worst – citing their sweatshops in Indonesia as an absolute disgrace regarding working conditions, salaries and overall treatment of staff. My pal **Esther** who works for a justice firm called **Children on the Edge** told me that only a berk would buy Nike after knowing the truth, and I couldn't argue with that. Talking of **berks**, we all shook our collective heads in anguish as those pratts at **SKY TV** moved our clash with **Burnley** to Monday night. Away supporters will be housed in the **David Fishwick** stand at Turf Moor –

this has to be the best named stand in football. The bloke sells minibuses in Lancashire. I'm sure you agree there's only one David Fishwick. Our next away game is against **Everton** at the end of the month. Goodison Park is one of my favourite away grounds – always a good atmosphere and its a little bit old school, do you know what I mean? Can't help but feeling nostalgic when squeezing through a rickety turnstile, stepping in puddles of urine in the bogs and having the privilege of a scouser making a cut-throat gesture across his neck to me – a customary welcome greeting as I step on his cherished Liverpudlian soil. A 5.30pm kick-off will ensure a **proper atmosphere** in the away end. As a **low-stake betting man**, I'm definitely popping a few coins on Burnley and Everton to score first against us. I'm a Chelsea **pessimist**, me.

September 2014:

Just the one PL away game in the month of September, against the champions **Manchester City.** My worst experience at the new Maine Road was freezing my nuts off one December evening when it was at least minus six degrees. I couldn't celebrate **Joey Cole's** winner as I was frozen solid. Even the coins bouncing off my head which had been Frisbeed at me by a Manc who looked like the lead singer of **Right Said Fred**, couldn't break the ice in my bones. Since moving on loan, **Sir Frank Lampard** could feature for City. If he does and ends up taking a corner by the away end, I fully expect the lower tier to launch themselves, as one, over the advertising hoardings and embrace the best player ever to represent our club. The game should be halted, of course, and only re-started once every supporter on the pitch has personally hugged and kissed their idol. My tip for this game is for **Eden Hazard** to leave **Zabaletta** on his arse seventeen times during the ninety minutes. And score two penalties.

October 2014:

Away games this month are at **Palace** and **Manchester United**. I actually haven't been to **Selhurst Park** since a pre-season friendly in 2003 (plastic) when **Geremi** scored a free-kick. That's about all I can recall. I can remember a bit more about my last trip to **Old Trafford** – a 2-2 draw in the FA Cup during the period when the chorizo loving waiter was unforgivably asked to 'manage' our glorious team. I travelled up by jumping on one of the **Squadron Leader's** 'famous' coaches and had to listen to **Tape Mix Tim's** musical compilation, that included tunes by the Lighthouse Family and Mark Morrison. Luckily I'd been boozing for about seven hours so I fell asleep on the way home so was saved from hearing those tunes on repeat again and again. October, for me, is always boosted by the fact that it is half-term. This means two things. The potential of taking one, or both, of my kids to the Bridge and also **buying a new pair** of trainers. It's been three months since August when the last new pair was purchased. When you have a baby and become a parent, you discover that **baby-wipes** are the best invention since someone decided mixing Smirnoff Ice with half a lager to create a pint of **Super-Shandy** – try it, if you dare. Anyway, back to the baby-wipes. I had my first child aged 32 years old. I instantly began using baby-wipes to clean my trainers. This was **definitely** the best thing about having kids and I was absolutely **kicking myself** for taking so long to discover them sooner. In fact, I'm amazed that **Adidas** haven't gone into partnership with Johnson & Johnson. Well, we all know that these days every man and his dog have a pair of **Gazelles** in their wardrobe, but hopefully if you've done your own research and begun boycotting Nike – now is the time to choose some new trainers, and I would suggest considering **Puma** or **Adidas** as your next pair – Ze German efficiency and all that, innit. Speaking of which, my **any time goalscorer** bets for both these matches will be on **Andre Schurrle** – go on, Mein Son.

November 2014:

PL away trips to **Anfield** and the **Stadium of Light** beckon this month. My **optimistic tip** is for **Torres** to score any time in both games – just watch me either reel in some top dollar or, more likely, hand over my Schurrle winnings from last month straight back to Patrick Power. When Gerrard scored an own goal in the 2005 **League Cup Final**, we thought it couldn't get any better. Then in 2007 in the CL, **Riise** scored an own goal in the last minute in front of the Kop, and once more we thought it couldn't get any better. Then, in 2010, we won 2-0 up there (**Drogba** scoring after a terrible Gerrard back pass) with **Carlo** in charge to virtually **clinch the league**, which officially came a week later when we smashed Wigan. Couldn't get any better, could it? Well, in 2014, Gerrard slipped and **Demba Ba** scored. A nation rejoiced. Let's hope for more of the same. Got a feeling the away end may well be serenading Brendan Rodgers with a song about a **tranny**. As for the **Sunderland** game, well at least it isn't on a weekday evening this season. Make sure you check the weather before you leave – some of the more cissy amongst us may well be giving their **long-johns** their first outing of the season. Brrrrrr.

December 2014:

"Feed the Scousers, let them know it's Christmas time." Ah, good old **Christmas.** A time when we all forget the fact that **Baby Jesus** was born into the world and instead get into ridiculous amounts of stress and debt by buying **material** gifts for people that will be forgotten about by Boxing Day. It can only mean one thing – time for a **new pair** of trainers. Its been

another three months since your last pair. This time, I suggest you mix it up with some **Asics** or **Diadora** on your feet. You then will have three pairs to rotate (Augusts, Octobers and Decembers pairs) to take you right through until the summer of 2015 when the process will start again. If baby-wipes aren't quite doing the trick these days, chuck your trainers in the **washing machine**. Trust me, I'm an expert. Wrap each trainer in a separate **pillow-case**, and tie a knot in the top. Put the washing machine on a **fast-wash thirty degree** cycle. Once washed, remove the pillow-cases and place your trainers either in the airing cupboard or balance them face down on the top of a radiator. **Good as new**. No need to thank me. You now have eight months until your next pair. Anyway, December is mental with six PL games this month, three away games feature – it is gonna be an expensive one. **Newcastle** will undoubtedly see loads of you stay over and burn the Queens Head in casinos and strip-joints. My advice would be avoid the strippers but stick a **bullseye on roulette red** and walk away with your winnings. None of you will stay the night over in **the Potteries**. The old slapper **Rihanna** once sang about **Finding Love in a Hopeless Place** – she has obviously never been to Stoke. A trip to **Southampton** at the end of the festive month awaits. The last time I went to St. Mary's I was 'treated' to an alcoholic concoction called a **Hiroshima** (the ingredients are a secret) by

@10Mar1905, and, true to its name, my head exploded. It was, as he described it, a game-changer. I missed half an hour of the **second half** and spilt **two balti pies** down my favourite jacket. My **betting tip** regarding the Saints is that **Ronald Koeman** will be the first manager to leave his post this season.

January 2015:

Ah, Tottenham away. Hatred and history. South London v North London. This is the first fixture most people look out for when the list comes out in June. A certain section of their lot will **still be fuming** after a mob of them got done in West Brompton before our game at the Bridge in March. Imagine larging it out the tube station and singing your songs while walking down the road, not realising there were three Chelsea pubs all within close vicinity that were rammed with lads getting tanked up before the 5.30pm kick off. We meet again. **Happy New Year.** Our next away game is against **Swansea.** Mid-January. Wales. Ball-boys. **You do the math.** My money is on a home win, I'm afraid. It's over six months away and I can still sense a defeat coming.

February 2015:

The best manager in the world, Jose, doesn't have a good record at **Villa Park**. When are this lot gonna go down? They're a right load of old flannel. The less said about Birmingham, the better, though we will

ALWAYS have: "**It was Villa away on the eleventh of May when Super Frankie he got the record!**" Next up away this month is **Leicester City**. My pal **Leicester Chris** who drinks Carling with a splash-of-lime down my local drives to every Foxes game. So that's me sorted for transport. Only thing, is that the game is currently scheduled to be played on my Doris's birthday. Oh well, **Chelsea was here before you were, love.** Besides, we got married on January 10th 2004 and I missed Chelsea winning 4-0 at the Walkers Stadium while I was posing for wedding photographs in a badly fitting suit. And I might be wrong, but I don't think we've played them up there since.

March 2015:

When we play **West Ham** it will be the **second-to-last-game** against them at **Upton Park**. You'll be reading / already read loads about the culture of the modern game, soul-less bowls and plastic seats, corporate clients and cheese-boards, a generation of supporters priced out and heavy handed stewards and (especially) Old Bill flexing their muscles outrageously because you are going to the football and they have a uniform or a luminous bib on. So, I won't bother adding my two pennies worth. Then its off to **Hull City**. Now, I'm getting on a bit. I'm all confused. Do we call them **The Tigers** now? Modern football, eh? I need a drink. My **prediction** for this game is a

comfortable win with a bet on four or more goals being scored by Chelsea.

April 2015:

It's Easter. Time to put your trainers in the washing machine. Don't forget the pillow-cases. Easter is a good laugh. There are a couple of **bank holidays** and that, and the clocks have changed meaning we embrace lighter evenings, the grass gets cut, and the scent of the coming summer begins to hang lightly on the breeze. In the Great British calendar, Easter is a time to remember when Jesus died on the cross and, three days later, rose again. These days we squeeze in as much football as possible and listen to the women in our life explain how well they've been dieting since the New Year so they're justified in going on a four-day-chocolate-egg-bender. On the pitch we meet **QPR** – don't forget that West London is theirs. When younger QPR fans give you the needle with taunts of *"Where Were You When You Were Shit?"* there is no need to rise to it. We were all over their ground. Every time. For example, there's a quite lovely photo taken in **1991** when we drew 2-2. **Wisey** has just equalized and in stoppage time and Chelsea are going mental all over. The YouTube footage of this match features a great moment after **Townsend** pulls a goal back – a Chelsea supporter runs on the pitch, ruffles the goalscorers hair, pats him on the back, and jogs back into the stand:

https://www.youtube.com/watch?v=PB0GI8px1pA I was in the side terrace that day (after getting separated from my mates on the way in) and can confirm that we had three sides of their ground. Townsend was our Captain. At home games, his name was the first sung when the players came out the tunnel: **Oh Andy Andy, Andy Andy Andy Andy Townsend**. He's not loved so much any more. We also play those unbearable pratts **'The' Arsenal** this month. If you don't lump on **Didier Drogba** to score then you've had a nightmare. It's also worth knowing that **Jose** has never lost a game to these muppets. Long may that continue. Make sure that you take as many **stickers** as possible to this match and plaster them all over their horrible ground.

May 2015:

The month of May sees us play three home games at the Bridge – our only away game is at **WBA**. The Hawthorns is is one of the grounds that I quite like. I dunno why. You can always get some **smashing food** in the Vine – and a decent **local ale** too. The away end is all right – not like at Molineux when you're all spread out along the side of the pitch. The Chelsea choir should all join together on sixteen minutes and sing **One Di Matteo –** because you'll probably find that most the home fans would agree.

And **that concludes** my preview of the season. Here are some final thoughts:

Refs:

If **Mike Riley** or **Mike Dean** are in charge of **ANY** of our matches, stick a little bet on **red cards** and **Chelsea to lose**. Just a hunch. Can't think where I've got that idea from.

Seasons' accessories:

If you don't have a **cfcuk fanzine** rolled up and stuffed in the back pocket of your jeans, you should be ashamed of yourself. You'll have nothing to read on the way home.

FA Cup Away fixtures:

The first thing to remember is to take plenty of **celery.** It's the FA Cup away, innit. Personally I hope we draw Fulham at some point. Putney Bridge, the Eight Bells, Bishops Park, the glorious Thames.

Juan Mata:

We don't burn shirts. We applaud returning players. Especially a man like Juan Mata. Oozing humility, wearing great clobber, our back-to-back player of the season, an exquisite footballer and an absolute gentleman. If **Neil Barnett** says anything of note this season, it should be to announce Mata's name as he jogs out of the tunnel at Stamford Bridge to embrace the resounding applause from the supporters who truly value him for all he did for Chelsea. You can heckle me for being a sentimental plonker – but I don't mind admitting that I miss Juan.

Stamford Bridge boozers:

For those who like an overpriced, flat, shitty lager in a plastic pint cup then you're spoilt for choice. For those who like a proper drink in a proper glass, just look a bit further afield. You'll find a more cultured supporter quaffing decent booze. Like my mate Smiffy, who looks like a Norwegian Fisherman.

Walking opportunities:

I love a good ramble. Yep, I've even got a pair of hiking boots. I know of several supporters that like to walk to different grounds. Walking is good for the soul. There are loads of brilliant walks in London. Try it with a mate or two. It makes a change. Often people are forced into this when we have a London match and there are transport problems, and realise that once they walked it, they quite liked it. So – take the opportunity this season to go *Strollin', just Strollin', with the light of the moon above, Ev'ry night I go out strolling, And I know my luck is rolling, When I'm strolling with the one I love – CHELSEA! CHELSEA!*

The Weather Forecast:

Do yourself a favour, and before each game remember to check the weather forecast via good old **@cliveoconnell** who poses as **Driver on the Wing** with **Alternative Weather Reports** on the **CSG** website: www.chelseasupportersgroup.net

Cheers for reading. Don't forget to wash your trainers on a thirty-degree cycle with each trainer wrapped separately in a pillow-case.

Disclaimer:

The author is not responsible for any losing bets you may place as a result of reading this piece. However, if you don't have a few quid on **Diego Costa** getting at least two red cards before the end of October, you're an idiot.

SUMMER TRANSFER WINDOW

IN:

Cesc Fabregas.

"Fabregas! Fabregas! Celery, is nothing to be scared of."

Diego Costa.

"Oh Diego Costa, he is a monster, he's fucking class. Coming from Madrid with Felipe and Courtois, banging in the goals with Eden and Oscar. Oh Diego Costa...."

Felipe Luis.

"There's only one Alexei Smertin."

Didier Drogba la-la-la-la-la.

Loic Remy.
"Stop your fooling around (ah-aaa-ah), better think of your future (ah-aaa-ah), there's a hole in your heart (ah-aaa-ah), Costa will always start (ahead of you) Remy. A message to you Remy."

Thibaut Courtois.
(Not even sure how to pronounce his name to be honest.)

OUT:

David Luiz You Were the Love of My Life; Samuel ("Hello, Hello!") Eto'o; Henrique Hilario; Jhon Pirez; Adam Mditi; Sam Hutchinson; Ashley Cole's won the European Cup; Lord Lampard; Demba Ba Superstar; Patrick Van Aaholt; Milan Lalkovic; Romelu Lukaku ("You're just a shit Emile Heskey."); Daniel Pappoe; George Cole; Billy Clifford; George Saville; Isak Sewankambo.

Forget arguments about loyalty points, selling Juan Mata, David Ellary in 1994 or corruption at FIFA – the biggest tragedy at Chelsea was the fact **Isak Sewankambo** never made the first team. Imagine the chants, the flags and the messages of adoration penned on (stained) sheets.

LOANED OUT:

Tomas Kalas; Wallace ("Cheeeese please, Gromit."); Christian Cuevas; Thorgan Hazard; Bertrand Traore; Mario Pasalic; Lucas Piazon; Ryan ("Ryan. Lion. Bayern.") Bertrand; Gael Kakuta; John Swift; Oriol Romeu; Joao Rodriguez; Kenneth Omeruo; Christian Atsu (Bless You.); Stipe Perica; Victor Moses ("He Parts The Red Sea."); Josh McEachran (Last seen tweeting about taking a nap or going for another 'cheeky' Nandos.); Marko (The German Messi) Marin; Patrick Bamford (Bridge, Fulham Road, SW6); Fernando Torres; Marco Van Ginkel; Nathaniel Chalobah; Islam Feruz; Matej Delac; Ulises Davila; Jamal Blackman; Todd Kane; Alex Davey.

EVERTON 3-6 CHELSEA SATURDAY 30TH AUGUST 2014

All Aboard the Berk Bus!

I am in a gloomy mood. It wasn't supposed to be like this. It *isn't* supposed to be like this. Since the fixture list came out, I've been buzzing for this – I have been *needing* this. My adrenaline went up a notch when the Squadron Leader announced he was putting on a coach for the lads. Now here I am drained and tired, head all fuzzy, walking across the pub floor to a find the toilet in a dead-end Wetherspoons somewhere in SW19 on Saturday morning, nine hours until kick off.

The lock is a bit busted on the cubicle door, but I sit down on the toilet anyway and get flustered with the toilet roll. It is twisted up inside the plastic holder and refusing to come out of the slot on the bottom. It is taunting me. Half eight on a Saturday morning, thirty lads full of fried breakfast and waiting patiently for the coach to appear out the front of the establishment, and I can't get the fucking toilet roll out its holder to wipe my arse. Although I have got time on my side, (which is the one silver lining in this whole episode) I am out of patience – I repeatedly punch the toilet roll holder then bury my head in my hands. I take a deep breath and try to pinch the end of the tissue to feed it through the slot, and finally and thankfully I manage it. Praise the Lord.

With my left hand I rub my eyes with my fore-finger and thumb. Last night I had a few hours of broken sleep on a mattress in Big Chris's living room, ready for the early start to get to Worcester Park to park the car then train it to this SW19 boozer. My Doris was back at home with the kids, texting me regularly through the night because she's had to get the paramedics out to see to our poorly daughter, and I should be there, I want to be there, but I dunno... it is what it is.

I've had two months of worry and frustration. My Doris has been recovering from surgery at the same time as my daughter suffering with on-going respiratory issues. So, you see, Everton away has been anticipated for weeks. You could say it is my summer holiday, seeing as my family hasn't had one. In all selfishness, today is supposed to be *my* day out and *my* time away – but then I wrestle with my thoughts because family is family and I'm not going to list my sacrifices, it's not like that, but you got to do what you've got to do, and sitting here on this bog and staring at the back of the cubicle door I feel weary and tired, so I prepare myself to get up and go to Wimbledon station and get the train home – and then my phone beeps again.

I pull my phone out of my pocket. I swipe my screen to unlock my phone and read a text from the Doris telling me to go to the game, my Mum is with them and helping out. She puts a few kisses on the end and signs off the text with the words *I love you* – I read the text over a few times, take another deep breath and lean back and think about my day ahead. It won't be long until I'm climbing the stairs on to the coach, patting the driver on the shoulder, ensuring I sit adjacent to Big Chris knowing that each mile the coach eats up on the motorway is a mile away from my responsibilities and how I've had to keep digging deep these last two months.

I put my phone in my pocket and exit the cubicle. I wash my hands while looking in the mirror, annoyed I didn't have my hair cut back, wondering if I've put the right polo on, I shake my head and dry my hands on the back of my jeans, pull open the toilet door and head past the bar to the front of the boozer, observing the lads gathered with no colours in sight, someone says, *here comes the coach,* off we bounce, here we go.

As I find a seat, guilt washes over me. I look at the text from the Doris again. I look up and smile at Big Chris – he is hauling a Sainsburys bag-for-life on to the coach – full of bottles of French lager that he has bought back from his family holiday in the Vendee region of France. He takes a seat adjacent to me, twists the red top off a green bottle and hands it to me. He twists the top off another bottle and we clink them together. I show him the text and he winks at me. I settle back in my seat and look out the window as the coach driver starts the engine.

A CD is handed up from the back towards the front, I take it and hold it at an angle, the shine of the silver glistens, no writing on it, a compilation of sorts, I walk to the front, I crouch by the driver, the hole in the player greedily swallows the disc, the volume turned to loud, *Baby Come Back* by The Equals kicks in – the buzz on the coach goes up a notch, the music accompanying the expectant, vibrant mood. I look down the coach all the way to the back and observe this loveable bunch: Ant the Cap, Ryan, The Sherman Chef and his Rosy Faced son, Fingers, Ross, The

Squadron Leader, Tape Mix Tim, Drews and his brother, Skip, Cal, Famous, Josh (for once without his boyfriend Beefy), Big Chris, Welsh James, loads of others, the list goes on, faces and names, Chelsea away games, ebb and flow, one season morphs into another, here we are once more.

Famous is reading the *Guardian* and Big Chris is doing a crossword from a puzzle pad that he brought with him. You've got a laugh. Showing their age. Cal pulls out a plastic cup from the top of a packet and hands it to me, the litre of Gin and the bottle of tonic soon follow. Why not. Here we go. *Cheers, Cal.* One gin follows the next and then the next. The Specials comes on and everyone is singing: *A Message to You Remy* – this is the life.

We pull into the services and cigarettes are greedily lit. The Doris rings me and I walk round in circles as she fills me in. My daughter has just had a chest x-ray, they've pumped her again with steroids but she's coping all right, it's for the best, I push my glasses off my nose and rest them on my head, the gin emphasises my tiredness rather than lifting it, and I feel all helpless like, my daughter on the x-ray table, the NHS no closer to knowing the underlying issue to her summer of illness, I'm helplessly marooned at a service station between Goodison Park and home, a match ticket in my pocket and circles round my eyes, four months to the day since my last game (30th April, Atletico Madrid at home), the Doris now asking me how I am and all of a sudden I well up then I hide it then I lie that I'm doing fine, darling, everything is great, thanks for encouraging me to go today and that.

A Club Coach pulls into the services and parks next to ours and No Beans Kenny hobbles off. He went to his first game in 1961 and I haven't seen him for exactly a year to the day, when I helped him up the steps to his seat in Prague for the Super Cup. We have a chat and I forget everything for a bit, then we're back on the coach and heading for a boozer outside Merseyside.

I explain to the fierce bar maid how to make a shot of Bakewell Tart. She ain't like the lovely treacles down the Finborough, in fact this moody cow couldn't be less accommodating. I explain patiently that it is half a shot of Disaronno, topped up with cherry juice (or Cranberry juice as a substitute) with a splash of lime cordial in the top. I order twelve shots, off she goes round the bar, I nod to the local geezer sitting on the stool next to me and ask him if they call her 'smiler' on account of her grumpy disposition. He looks at me and tells me that she is his missus. I apologise and offer my hand. He shakes it. She brings the shots on a tray and puts them on the bar with a scowl. I put two shots in front of the geezer. One for him. One for her. I walk away with the tray in my hands, finding all the lads outside I tell them to help themselves, quickly necking one for myself first as their hands dive in for theirs.

The Squadron Leader and Tape-Mix Tim appear with a tray of jager-bombs. Ant the Cap has put his flag up. Someone starts the *Brendan Rodgers* song. *"Brendan Rodgers left his wife to go and shag a tranny, pulled her knickers to the side, she didn't have a fanny."* Those who witness Big Chris doing the actions choke a little on their lagers.

Finally, we pull up outside Goodison. I stand at the front of the coach with a bin liner, the chaps popping their empties in as they file off. Once the lads have gone I jump down onto the pavement to find the Fulham Old Bill greeting me as I step off, and suddenly my back is to the wall. Goggles is firing questions at me with his note book in his palm. *No, I didn't organise this coach. No, I don't know who did. I was collecting rubbish, officer.* Big Chris stands with his arms folded next to me. As Goggles goes through my wallet, I stare at the side of the coach and pray under my breath, wondering if I can catch a break for once this summer, if that's all right. He only lets me go after I give him my real name and my membership number. Thankfully, nothing comes of it, though we learn later that the coach driver grassed up the actual organiser and, later in September, all those on the Berk Bus chip in to cover the fine he receives for commandeering the coach.

Outside Goodison I finally meet Tom and Lizzi and hand over their match tickets which I've had in my pocket for them all day long. We just make kick-off. Costa 1-0. Ivanovic 2-0. Shout, shout, let it all out.

Only a few minutes of the second half has ticked by when I hear a cry of anguish. Famous has gone over on his ankle. I help him up. A steward takes us to first aid. They help him on to a bed and they unlace his trainer. Bruising and swelling appear before my eyes. Ice is packed around his ankle.

I ask a paramedic to show me to the toilet. I go for a piss. I come out. St John's have bandaged Famous's ankle. I take him back to his seat. We didn't miss any goals. At full time the Chelsea players walk over, applauding and *OLE OLE OLE OLE, CHELSEA, CHELSEA* rings out. Marvellous. I look at John Terry as I applaud back – I bumped into him a few weeks ago in Cobham High Street. (Well, I say *bumped into*, I actually chased after him and called his name.) He stopped and chatted. Meant the world to me. It's well strange to talk to a hero – I mean, I've sung his name up and down the country and in Europe – and suddenly he is asking me how I'm doing and all that and my mouth went dry and I couldn't really say much.

I sleep for a lot on the coach back. My lack of kip and the booze has taken over. When we arrive back in SW19, the Squadron Leader wakes me up I dawdle up to the taxi rank with Big Chris to get a cab to Worcester Park to kip at his sister's gaff. We jump in a taxi and the cab driver is telling us that we played more flowing football under Rafa. It's probably the worst ever ending to a day I've ever had. Rafa? Do me a favour! Then I remember a message I read on my phone earlier. Two Chelsea pals have transferred some money into my account under strict instructions to pay for a baby sitter and take the Doris out for a decent meal. Chelsea away and mates. The glue that holds it all together.

REGENERATE AND THE CHELSEA SUPPORTERS GROUP (CSG)

Regenerate was born in January 2000, based on the Alton Estate in Roehampton. It was founded by Andy Smith who, at the time, was a season ticket holder in the MHL. Andy was working in the Robert Joy Day Centre in Putney – a Lunch Club for pensioners in the area, who had a sudden influx of new members from Roehampton because their local Lunch Club has been closed by the council due to local cuts. The situation inspired Andy (with his mum Mo) to set up a new charity to raise funds, acquire donations and re-launch the Lunch Club. After a few successful weeks running the new project, Andy became increasingly aware of the needs of the young people on the Estate. There was no provision for them. Truancy, crime and anti-social behaviour thrived. For many, a pathway to dealing, gangs, young offenders and prison had become the norm. I had been a Youth Worker in Epsom, Ewell and Worcester Park for about six years as was feeling like I needed a change. Down the boozer before a home game one day in early 2000, I decided to jump ship and work for Andy and set up Youth Work on the Estate for 8 to 14 year olds with the support of a bunch of enthusiastic, committed volunteers. The nuns in the local convent donated Andy the money to pay my first months wages.

Fast forward to March 2013. I had written a book called *The Red Hand Gang* published by GATE17. Much of the book focused on the early years of Regenerate. We held a book launch at the *Star and Garter* in Putney, raising about £400 for Regenerate via the raffle. A load of my Chelsea pals were in attendance, including Cliff Auger of the CSG. During the launch, Luke Clifford was interviewed about how the support of Regenerate had helped him in his life. This was intended to inspire all those who were at the launch that their donations would go to significant use. Visibly moved by his story, Cliff, on behalf of the CSG, asked if Regenerate would be happy to be the beneficiary of funds raised via the annual Supporters Tournament at Cobham. Of course! Representing Regenerate because Andy was away, I was fortunate enough to go on the Stamford Bridge turf before the Palace game on Saturday 14th December 2013 and receive a cheque for £500. It was the first time I had been on the pitch since invading it in 1994 after we beat Wolves in the FA Cup Quarter Final.

This season, before the Villa match at the Bridge, Andy and young Zac Jervis were on the pitch with the CSG's Liz Nurse to receive a £400 donation. Zac is 8 years old and the grandson of our good mate Den. Den has been hugely supportive (behind the scenes) of Regenerate's work, especially in the early years. As you can imagine, Zac was over the moon to be on the pitch. After the presentation, he was spotted by Mark Schwarzer who gave him a pair of his goalie gloves – a splendid gesture. Zac then promised to pass these on to his best mate (who is a goalkeeper) – what a wonderful thing for both Mark and Zac to do.

All the staff, volunteers and beneficiaries at Regenerate want to say a huge thank you to all those who took part in the Supporters Tournament in 2013 and 2014 and to the CSG for their generosity.
Read more about Regenerate via their website. www.regenerateuk.co.uk
Twitter: @regenerateuk

CHELSEA 3-0 ASTON VILLA SATURDAY 27TH SEPTEMBER 2014

The Walk of Glory

My alarm goes off and I wake up with a smile, kick myself out of bed, cross the landing, check on the sleeping kids, jump in the shower and remind myself to find my pin badge in the pot above the fire-place. I hate forgetting it. My walk to the train station is just over a mile, the weather is mild, no sign of summer disappearing, the evenings are kicking in quicker these last couple of weeks, but its still been a shirt-with-no-jacket-required type of weather.

There's a different sort than usual working in the small café by the level-crossing. I wait by the side window and watch her turn bacon with her left hand

and crack an egg in the pan with her right – I say *hello* and as she turns her head I stick my order in and politely mention that I have eight minutes until my train (it's actually ten) – she smiles back and says, *no problemo,* even though she definitely isn't Spanish.

It is going to be two hours until my next cigarette, so I step back and light up. I'll try quitting again after today, I promised the kids I would. It isn't hard for me to decide to give it another go – not when my daughter has terrible asthma – yesterday she was back in A&E again with an oxygen-mask over her face, and I listen to the Respiratory Specialist explaining to me that even though I don't spark up in the house or near the kids, the state of my skin and clothes after smoking is still enough for her to be breathing in chemicals that affect her chest – they are silently and invisibly poisoning her as I read her a bed-time story or help her with her spellings for school or walk her to the shops to spend her pocket money on penny sweets and princess magazines.

The train pulls up and I do the thing I always do – select a carriage where I can sit by a window and have the back of a chair in front of me rather than a table – for too many years now I have had random eccentrics sitting opposite me. I seem to attract them – usually some bizarre fellow with a quirky name and a passionate interest in an odd hobby will inevitably latch on and give me ear-ache – this is why I choose to sit where I do these days – in the corner next to a window at a seat with no table – it is about me with my thoughts – shutting the week out, my phone turned off, the train limping along the coast from one station to another before joining four more carriages at Haywards Heath – I might have a slight doze, I might not – the main thing is though I won't be getting irritated with a random perched opposite me pontificating about something tedious.

I change at Clapham Junction, platform five, and jump on the train to Putney. As I alight and walk towards the station, it appears to me that it's renovation is complete. The scaffolding has gone, the temporary walk-ways demolished – I step out into a mild and cheery South West London Saturday morning and I stop for a second to lean against the wall, light a cigarette and observe the scene buzzing around before me:

Cars beep at each other; Polish drivers floor their red double deckers into Upper Richmond Road; Mothers adorned in Lycra speed-walk their buggies past pubs and cafés; Couples point at the photos in Estate Agent windows; A man in a suit strides out of the bank; An elderly lady shuffles out of the Newsagents; A red nosed gentleman pushes into a betting shop; A sprinkle of Chelsea fans to my right trot out of the train station and cross the road, seeking to start their pre-match boozing at ten in the morning. I follow them.

I cross the road and push into the Railway. The barman from Dundee in Scotland is eating a curry, keen to tell me about his team the Tangerines and how life was so much better in the past before the TV money and foreign owners – I've heard it all before – but this is better than being at home and hanging a round of washing on the line to dry with another already turning in the machine, it never stops at the weekend – another cycle, hang it up, fill the drum with another load, repeat.

I order a large breakfast with an orange juice and extra toast and also a pint. A sign behind the bar tells me that 2,167 pints of ale had been served last week. Roger England and Pert, the Sherman Chef and Sal are all here now, but Smiffy is running late. We push on towards East Putney tube without him, the Fin is opening at eleven. The early booze tingles my brain, working its way through my bloodstream, pushing out the toxins of the week – my unwell daughter; the prick at work trying to make my business his business; a bill to pay; a habit to kick. Images on the news of a missing girl are dominating the news, her hair tied back, her last walk by the river recorded on CCTV, a Latvian monster took her life, no doubt she experienced pain beyond measure, this life, sometimes I wonder what it is all about.

I shake my head, try and think of something else. I close my eyes and feel the sun on my face, I listen to Roger and Pert talk about their trip to Lisbon and tales of untold Caipirinha cocktails – Roger says they came home more lime than human. I laugh at the Sherman Chef trying to solve a puzzle on the East Putney platform – we are West Brompton bound – laughter and mates, the pub and old friends, Stamford Bridge, win-lose-or-draw I'm not sure if I care right now, this moment is enough, I ain't been here at the Bridge since the 30th April and today is the 27th September.

It feels good to have a drink in The Fin. Smiffy turns up and hands me a cheese and ham sandwich. I stuff it in my pocket for later. After a few pints it is time for us to begin, what we call, the Walk of Glory. I have no idea why or how we coin in like this, but we have. We turn left out of the Fin and walk to the off licence to pick up a few cans of Gin and Tonic and Bacardi and Coke. We pop our cans and pass Brompton Cemetery to our left then West Brompton Station. We stroll over the bridge and wave at the drinkers we know boozing outside the Wee Imp before turning left down Seagrave Road. There is a perfect little spot to relieve the bladder should one need to go, and then we take a right to come out on Farm Lane. We pass the Fox pub on our left – drinkers spill out on to the pavement and we raise a can to those we know. We come out at the Malster to be faced with a choice. We either turn right to go and drink in the Cock, or turn left into Fulham Broadway to stroll down to the stall. Today we turn right.

We nod at the bouncers outside the Cock and step inside. Smiffy goes to the bar and I go out into the beer garden to pick up my ticket from Sausage Rolls. Mad Gray has got a new pair of trainers on and he tells me all about his summer. After a quick drink we leave the Cock, cross the road by the church and head down the Fulham Road to the stall. There we meet Kenny Christmas to pick up Smiffy's ticket. It feels good to be here. The crowds are building. The weather is better-than-mild. Den and Zac turn up. Zac is absolutely buzzing to know he'll soon be on the pitch with Smiffy to receive a £400 cheque for Regenerate from the CSG.

I get into the ground early – easily the earliest I've been in for maybe a decade or more, I'm sure. A plastic bottle of London Pride sets me back £4.20. Gourlay's coffers are further boosted while my pockets fall into the overdraft. Easy come, easy go. I'm in my MHU seat by 14:35 – I watch the pitch as Smiffy and Zac take to the turf and I take a photo of the big screen as their faces beam with gratitude. Zac is clearly over the moon. At half-time and I meet up with Taxi Alan, Vastly Intelligent Keef and Tax-Dodging Tommy. Another season, another day, more flecks of silver in each of our hair and stubble – the voice of my Aunty Sue comes into my head telling me that going grey is a sign of wisdom, I won't argue with that! I make my way back to my seat ten minutes into the second half, tuts of annoyance from the row who have to stand to let me through, they're riled at me for inconveniencing them by making them stand – I am late and they are moaning, oh well, tick-tock, don't get your mega-store pants in a twist, life goes on.

After the game I come out of the ground and bump straight into Cathy. We go to La Reserve for one with Phil the Butler. There's Slough Jon and Mince Pie getting bang on it. I stay for one and decide to return to the Fin where Smiffy is heading. Though the vast crowds have dispersed, Smiffy and I sack off the tube option and walk all the way on my own – the reverse Walk of Glory. I reflect on the game: The speed and balance of Hazard; Willian all nippy and feisty; Costa belonging in a Spaghetti Western; the astonishing leadership of John George Terry – I chew all of this over – Chelsea are top of the league, there is a long way to go, but I reckon that this season could be very special.

It is nearly seven o'clock but the weather is still brilliantly mild. I suddenly feel very hungry. I dig out the crumpled cheese and ham sandwich that has been in my pocket since midday. I stay at the Fin for a bit but I've got to make a stag-do in Brighton – I promised I'd be there for dinner in a restaurant on the sea-front – it is on my way home, anyway. My thoughts become dark and murky now, the booze throughout the day now pressing my buttons; be-headings in Syria; the Tories ignoring the cry from the poor; Melanie Shaw (google her) banged up in Nottingham; the Rotherham nonces no closer to jail – I try to push these thoughts away to return to being bright and optimistic – the train pulls up at Clapham to take me to Brighton – the carriages are rammed but I'm lucky to find a seat.

It is a table seat. I shuffle in and sit down, accidentally kicking the passenger opposite me because his legs are stretched out under the table. I look up and smile an apology. A man with wild, white hair smiles and – worse than that – he nods a firm welcome at me. I instantly find myself saying *hello.* He looks like Doc from *Back to the Future*. He tells me his name is Bruce. And that he is retired. And that he has been to London to look at motorbike parts. I have no reply. I think my mouth is wide open. Suddenly, the unmistakably welcome noise of the squeaky wheels of a drinks trolley resounds down the aisle. I raise my hand and order two cans of Strongbow. I pass one over the table to Bruce. The cans cost £3.30 each. Maybe Ron Gourlay is in charge of these prices, too. The person to Bruce's left adjusts the headphones in her ear and stares down at her tatty book. I pop the ring-pull on my cider, raise my can to Bruce and ask him to tell me all about his day. I drink long and drink deep before settling back as Bruce the Eccentric leans forward and begins to enthusiastically describe to me the intricacies of certain motorbike parts.

To be honest, I couldn't care less. I just want to get to Brighton to my mates stag do. However, I feel I must be polite and take interest. My meeting-an-eccentric--random-on-the-train has happened, so I shall sip my drink and let it unravel. As I listen to Bruce, it crosses my mind that I am probably eccentric in my own way – I mean, imagine titling a match-day stroll from one pub to another as *The Walk of Glory*.

CHELSEA 2-1 QPR SATURDAY 01ST NOVEMBER 2014

Where were you when the phones had twisty cords?

It is the morning of the first of November. I am on a train to Brighton to meet Smiffy and Seagull Si where we'll connect to go to Seaford. From Seaford we will walk to Eastbourne.

We book in a few hikes each year. Back in June we walked 16 miles from Brighton to Seaford, got blisters and sunburn, ate a curry and got on the beers with Seaford based @carl_344, proper old school Chelsea. Today we're completing the next leg, fifteen or so miles from Seaford to Eastbourne, and in some ways it is a special occasion as we are marking the tenth anniversary of walking one hundred miles of the

River Thames. Back in 2004, Seagull Si, Smiffy and I walked 20 miles a day for five days. Back then we were all aged 29, about to hit 30. We talked about our age a lot – you know, thoughts about turning 30 years of age. As the magnificent River guided us from Oxford to Richmond, we chatted and reflected on our twenties being left behind, (which formed the backbone for my book *The Red Hand* Gang), and now here we are, a decade on, soon to hit our naughty forties.

I step off the train at Brighton to wait for the other two to arrive and I take a moment to watch. I observe people queuing for tickets at booths, people queuing for tickets at machines, people queuing for cash at walls, people queuing as they stare up at electronic departure boards, people queuing to go through barriers. All this scene does is make me long for the impending solitude of walking, of nature and of quiet.

Maybe I need solace.

I take my phone out and turn it on, load up an app called *Map my Hike* and think about how mad it is that every step I take on today's fifteen mile walk will be tracked by GPS. After each mile is completed, a lady with a lovely voice pipes up to inform me how long the mile took me and how quickly (or slowly) each mile, on average, takes me to walk. I need my battery to last me. If it dies, then I'll never know how many miles I've walked, how many steps I've taken, the exact route I hiked or how long it took me. Chelsea play QPR at 3pm, I'll have to rely on Si and Smiffy to give me updates from the Bridge via their phones, as mine will only be in use to track our adventure today.

Then, that got me thinking. When I was younger, before social media existed, before mobile phones had been invented, before the red button on the BBC was an option, before Jeff Stelling and *Soccer Saturday* exploded into action, it was so much different in terms of finding out the scores and results. House phones had long, twisy cords that stretched across a whole room. It almost feels like another life away. It was different for each person. Many supporters of a certain vintage would, on their way home, purchase the *Pink Paper* at major train stations detailing the days sporting events and results. This is how it was for me:

1) If Radio 2 sport coverage (now essentially what Radio 5 is now) covered a Chelsea game (highly unlikely) then I would listen to that in my bedroom.
2) If Radio 2 were covering another game (which they basically always were) I would listen to the featured game and have teletext

on the TV updating the other scores, naturally including the Chelsea game. Once I realised Capital Gold covered all the London teams throughout the divisions (back when Jonathan Pearce was the bees knees) I tuned into them. I always found Alan Green an irritant. Nothing has changed.

3) Sometimes if I was out (family stuff or a wedding, for example) I would go the whole day without knowing any scores and wait for *Match of The Day*. The wait was often worth it, watching highlights of every game not knowing any results – any piece of footage could inevitably lead to a goal, it was edge-of-the-seat stuff. (Though in my case, I often sat on a bean-bag.)

4) If I was at Stamford Bridge, then the place would fall quiet at half-time as we awaited the scores to be read out, and then again at full-time. The biggest cheers always came if the announcer confirmed that Tottenham had lost.

5) If I was on my way back from the

> Bridge and I saw fans from other teams at Wimbledon station, I'd always ask them how they got on. Likewise, others would ask me how Chelsea had done. Often these would be fellow Chelsea supporters who hadn't been at the game and had missed hearing the result on the radio. Unless the match was goal-less, the next question was always: "Who scored for us?"

Now, my memory isn't the best, but I honestly can't recall being at the Bridge and reading the half-times and full-times on the electronic scoreboard above the away end, I always heard them being announced over the PA system. Then, it struck me that, during the second half at games at the Bridge these days, the announcement, *"Today's attendance is 41,765 – thank you for your support!"*, has been read out by the same bloke for *years*! I'm sure it is the same voice NOW that was THEN! If Chelsea are losing, he definitely sounds disappointed when saying what the attendance is. If Chelsea are winning, his announcement is considerably more cheery.

(Later that week I was grateful for Chelsea Historian @RickGlanvill replying to my email to confirm: "The stadium announcer/DJ is usually Carl Chapman. I spoke to him yesterday and he said he's not quite sure when he started but it is *'definitely more than twenty years ago!'* I'm pretty sure in Bates' time the scoreboard that Leeds killed carried scores/results.")

My thoughts are interrupted as Si and Smiff turn up and we jump on the train to Seaford. By 10.00am we have left Seaford station and walk to the beach. We stare out at the English Channel for a few seconds until Si is the first to move. He turns left and starts to walk – fifteen miles to Eastbourne.

For hikers, this section of East Sussex is a popular walk. The path takes you over the famous *Seven Sisters* cliffs and Beachy Head. Indeed, when approaching Beachy Head, Si goes a bit batty and pretends he is on a moped and vrooms down the grass. He whistles the chorus to *"I've Had Enough"* by The Who and shouts over his shoulder that he is Jimmy in *Quadrophenia.* I pause for a moment, letting the others go ahead. I wonder how many people have jumped lately. Maybe last night. Maybe someone tonight. I look nervously around, seeing if I spot anyone looking slightly depressed. There is no-one. I find myself shuddering slightly. I remember reading an interview with a helicopter pilot who described how the finger nails on victims are often ripped away and covered in chalk where they have slid down the cliff and maybe grabbed for survival in a effort to claw their way back, but gravity takes over and it's too late as life comes to an abrupt end. I make a mental note to donate to *The Samaritans* and start jogging to catch up my walking comrades.

Though I could feel blisters forming on my toes, I said nothing. None of us spoke for a while. All of us had grown silent as we hiked past the last section of Beachy Head. As we began the descent down towards the promenade, we knew we'd meet the hustle and bustle of seaside life for the first time since Seaford.

We descend down to sea level and walk towards the promenade. Smiffy pulls out his phone out of his pocket and lets out a laugh. He tells us that in the early kick-off, Newcastle had beaten Liverpool. Result! Smiffy and I sing the *Brendan Rodgers* song a few times over, including the 'action' of pulling-the-kickers-to-the-side, followed by a waggling-finger, which Big Chris initiated on the Berk Bus back when we played Everton.

For the first time that day, I was suddenly aware of the temperature dropping and a swell of clouds in the sky. November the First and I've been wearing shorts and a T-shirt in very mild weather, but now it was time for the shower-proof jacket. As I shivered, Si checked his phone for directions. I checked my phone to see how far we had walked, but the battery hadn't lasted and my phone was dead. I was absolutely livid. It was important to me to have every step accounted for, the precise distance and mileage recorded on the counter and the exact duration of our hike on the clock. It had all been wasted. Smiffy empathised by handing me a cigarette.

On the promenade we watched an elderly man trying to roller-blade. He was wearing elbow pads, knee pads and an ill-fitting crash helmet. He was struggling for balance, was red in the face from exhaustion and drawing laughter from the people watching. He spent a lot of time gripping the bar running alongside the promenade to keep himself from falling over. We all laughed, if not inwardly mocking him slightly, but the more I watched him, the more something didn't add up. I watched him stop by a rubbish bin. He leant over it to pause for breath and gather himself together somewhat.

–You okay, mate? I ask him.

–Yes, yes, I think so.

–You a bit out of practice?

–You could say that. I've never done it before!

–Is it on your bucket list to master before,

you know, you get older?

He looked at me and smiled. He wobbled a bit before replying.

–My daughter used to roller skate here all the time when she was a child. I recently lost her. In a few months I'm raising money for *Cancer Research* by doing a sponsored roller skate up and down the promenade. I'm practising.

He smiled at me with both sorrow and pride. His eyes were moist. I could tell he was desperate to master it.

I held out my right hand. He took it and we shook firmly. I briefly glanced out to sea, focused on the horizon and patted the back of his hand with my left one. Then I let go and I dug in my pocket. All I could find was a measly two pound coin. I placed it in his palm and left him there, wobbling by the litter bin.

I crossed over the road. Seagull Si nodded towards the boozer which stood in its fine glory at the end of the road. We settled down with pints of Guinness. It was well past 3pm. We watched *Soccer Saturday* with Jeff Stelling and his crew. When Hazard prepared to take his penalty they went live to the commentary and

Smiffy and I punched the air and got another pint in to celebrate his goal.

The battery on Si's phone was still going strong. He fired up *National Rail Enquires* and planned our train from Eastbourne to Brighton. His beloved Seagulls were kicking off at 5.15pm away to Bournemouth. We drank up, got the train on time, got to Brighton and piled into a boozer showing the football. Plenty of Brighton fans filled the pub. As everyone focused on the game, I thought about yesteryear. We never needed an app to tell us the train times or if there were delays, we just knew when to leave. If we were late, we'd wait for the next one. If there was a delay, we'd deal with it. Life seemed simpler back then. Whether it was or not, I guess it doesn't matter anymore.

I thought about one time, maybe twenty years ago, when we'd all piled down to Hayling Island for a weekend away. About eight of us were staying in one of those massive, static vans. We all agreed with our Saturday morning hangovers that we'd try and get through the day without knowing any scores, and wait until *Match of the Day* started so we could watch the games unfold. We managed it. I can remember us all gathered around a small TV with a crate of cheap lager saying: *"We ain't done this in YEEAAARS!!!"*

Back in this Brighton boozer the South Coast derby was proper end-to-end stuff. We leant on the bar and watched the game, discussed our day, the pretty bar-maid and the landlord taking notice. The Bournemouth manager looks like he should still be doing a paper-round. However, I was finding it hard to focus. The day was taking its toll on me – the walk, the sea-air, the eerie feeling at Beachy Head, my lack of drinking practice and the discomfort caused by blisters were ushering me to leave the boozer and get myself back home. I said *goodbye* to the lads, winked at the pretty bar-maid, nodded to the landlord and walked to the station. It was only two minutes until my train home. Perfect. Sometimes having a dead phone battery is highly stressful. At other times, to be honest, it is rather liberating.

I take a seat and the train begins to pull away. I think about my childhood house phone with its white buttons and its beige twisty cord on a table in the hallway. I recite the phone number under my breath. I think about my Granny's big dial-phone. It was a mushy pea green colour and it sat by her musty, floral chair in her lounge. I struggle to recall her phone number and this frustrates me. I reckon my big sister would remember. I begin to fall asleep in my seat with my head resting on the back of the chair in front. I recall how I used to wrap the long twisty cord absent-mindedly around my finger when chatting to a mate on the phone. After the call my Dad would yell at me for twisting up the cord and my Mum would spend ten minutes unravelling it to how it should be.

I wonder if I would ever again spend a day not knowing any results and switching on *Match of the Day* to see the games and the scores unfold. Probably not. Things have changed so much. Now, your phone is mobile, it is your diary, your weather report, your traffic update, your digital radio, your music collection, your photograph album, your cinema and your television. You can even talk to your phone and it will talk back to you. Times have changed, they are changing swiftly, the revolution too fast for many. I close my eyes. I find myself thinking about the old boy wobbling on his roller-blades on the promenade at Eastbourne. Maybe I can search for his fund-raising page on social-media.

I instinctively pull my phone out my pocket before remembering the battery is dead.

CHELSEA 2-0 WBA SATURDAY 22ND NOVEMBER 2014

Love not war, and flowers

A couple of weeks before this game, I get an email from a Scandinavian fella called John who works for Norway TV. Says he's been on the *Chelsea Supporters Group* website and seen the article I wrote about Smiffy / @regenerateuk and Zac being on the Stamford Bridge turf pre-Villa. John says he wants to do an interview. I do a bit of homework on him, chat with Smiffy, we both feel chilled about it, so I email him back and say okay.

Two days before the game I go to SW15 and meet John and his cameraman Olly on the Alton Estate, Roehampton. It is a clear, but a cold day. We sit on a bench outside the shops and do an interview – the old bench has been bolted firmly down into the concrete – I bet it could tell a story. There's puke by my feet and litter blustering all around the car park by the small parade of shops. There is a small Londis one end of the parade, and a large Londis at the opposite end. In between there is a Chinese take-away with a giant fish tank that always needs a clean, next is Smiffy's office / youth drop-in centre, and then a barbers that is now shut-down. It used to be a front for a crack-den (to be fair, they cut decent hair as well cutting drugs) – before it was a barbers it was a grocers called *MARY D's FRUIT & VEG* and that prompts me to think about eating my five-a-day especially after boozing too much with Smiffy when I met him in Putney last night.

It crosses my mind that things like this (putting yourself on film) is a risk. I could get proper annihilated on social-media by all sorts. It's a gamble telling a story, making your feelings known, a sense of vulnerability, so maybe I'll post a link of the footage, maybe I won't. After I've finished I make a couple of calls, and then watch Craig as he leans against a tree on the green against a back-drop of eighteen floors of concrete. He has his hands dug deep in his pockets as he answers John's questions, his gaze avoiding Olly's camera, he's pretending it isn't there, I'm out of ear-shot but I notice he's shrugging his shoulders, telling

John how it is.

When Smiffy does his interview we're in the warm, coffee and sofas, heating on, door closed, estate noise shut outside. I listen and reflect that if this whole thing raises the profile of Regenerates work then mission accomplished, job done, block the cynical feedback, avoid the conflict, head down, move on, move upwards. We've got Saturday to come – John and Olly plan to finish their piece on the Fulham Road by the *cfcuk* stall – they'll meet the fanzine lot, the authors, the CST, the CSG – the camera running for ages – plenty of footage, a multitude of interviews, the documentary editor will have a right job on his hands.

On the day of the game I get an early train to Putney. I'm not going home tonight. I'm off to the in-laws in Cobham to stay the night. It's mother-in-laws birthday and we have a family do tomorrow. I push through the doors into the Railway Pub and order their largest breakfast. Smiffy texts that he's over-slept, but then Roger England waddles in so at least I've got some company. My food arrives. It looks terrible. It tastes even worse. It is cold and dry. I force it down. I'm never eating in here again. We walk to East Putney tube with a spring in our step, the District Line is up the spout but thankfully we're not affected. We get to the boozer and I'm bang on a lovely red ale called *LOVE NOT WAR* brewed by @LdnFldsBrewery – marvellous stuff. Jeff the landlord tells me that it's a brooding red ale – a silky texture – an ode to all things peace and love – it makes me think of something so I grab a pen and write *FLOWERS* in big, black letters on the back of my hand.

John and Olly turn up, talk to the landlord and then they film Immigrant Dan's tattoos – blimey, they must be desperate for footage. We call a cab to take us to the stall. Olly films this too. The driver is old-school Chelsea, full of praise for Hazard and Costa then when he begins reminiscing about the late sixties and early seventies, it is brilliant stuff. At the stall, once all the introductions and filming is done, Smiffy finally turns up and we leg it to the Fulham Tup because we are both thirsty. We drink 'til half two then go and meet a fella at the Peter Osgood statue for our tickets – I had luckily come across him that morning selling two for face value in the MHL. The brass-band are marching and playing *Blue is the Colour* as we queue to get in. I like this. We meet mates and booze together on the MHL concourse. This is the life. In the ground, my view wasn't great but I don't mind, the atmosphere was all right, too. One has to cherish moments like these. Top of the League, pace, movement, clinical play, job done, three points.

We've heard the Old Bill have put restrictions on the amount of people allowed to drink in the Wee Place, so we head to La Reserve for one after the game. As the crowd outside dies down as they make their way home, we see a few faces, have a catch-up, gulp from over-priced plastic bottles of Stella, push outside to the back section and spark up another cigarette. Smiffy and I decide to stay for a bit and then decide to return to the Fin. That red ale is calling me, beckoning me to return. We decide not to walk and jump on the tube instead. The pub is full, loads are watching a game on the box, but I don't care about that, we are the Chelsea and we are the best, someone pushes a fresh pint in my palm – *LOVE NOT WAR* – down it goes, I order another.

I knew it was time to stop boozing and leave the Fin after I popped down to the cellar to interrupt the *Chelsea Supporters Trust* meeting with a song about being Top of the League. (I texted apologies the next day to everyone I could think of). I get the District Line to Wimbledon and buy food and water. I get an SW train to Cobham and begin to walk a few miles to the High Street. Walking is good for the soul, and I could do with sobering up a bit. I pull my phone out of my pocket and I check on the time on my phone. It is then that I see the black writing on the back of my hand from this morning. I nip into Sainsburys and make a purchase.

I walk the length of the High Street and find the restaurant I'm looking for where I know my mother-in-law is having a birthday meal. I flick my cigarette towards the gutter, open the restaurant door and wait for the waitress to spot me. She steps forward to greet me and I hand her the flowers. I describe my mother-in-law, the waitress knows who I mean, which doesn't surprise me at all, because my mother-in-law has wild, curly, blonde hair. I ask the waitress to give her the flowers and wish her a happy birthday from her favourite son-in-law.

With my duties done, I stroll up the road towards the in-laws gaff knowing my kids will be in asleep in the spare room and the Doris will be sipping wine with her sisters. It's been a great day. I turn the final corner, the house only seven doors away and sing, *We're Top of the League, We're Top of the League* for the rest of the way.

NEWCASTLE 2-1 CHELSEA SATURDAY 06TH DECEMBER 2014

I am a criminologist

It is early in the morning and Big Chris and I are at the bus stop in Worcester Park. I dig my hands deeper into my pockets, it's five past six or something stupid like that, my breath is hanging in the air slightly before dispersing, we are waiting for Stan to turn up. There are a couple of other blokes wrapped up like Eskimos, shifting their feet, they've been there a while, two pairs of socks on, toes still feeling numb, here comes Stan, *good morning all*, the X26 bus to Heathrow is imminent – here it is now coming down the High Street, I take two quick pulls on my cigarette, flick the butt into the gutter, follow Stan up through the door and up the steps of the bus, push my Oyster card against the reader, wait for it to beep green, nod to the driver, walk to the back of the bus, find a seat, off we go.

(GATE 17 note: It is worth acknowledging that at £1.50 it is a widely held belief of the North Surrey Mafia that the X26 is the best value bus ride in the United Kingdom.)

It is so early the traffic is light, the bus takes no time at all: New Malden, Kingston, Teddington, Hatton Cross. When we jump off the bus, Stan helps a pretty air hostess by carrying her heavy suitcase down the steps. Stan asks her where she is going, she tells him she is off to Dubai, she blushes slightly, Stan has still got it, the cheeky flirt grins at us all victorious like as we head for the check-in.

Airports. They've changed. I hate all of this. I get all anxious. My phone doesn't even have that NFC function (or whatever it's called) to check in. A British Airways employee takes pity on me (whereas Big Chris and Stan take the piss out of me) when I pull a load of papers out of my pocket (that I printed out yesterday) and finally I have checked in and we head for the restaurant to order a breakfast.

Scott and Campo turn up with pints of lager in their hands. But there's no booze for me just yet, I have to learn from my mistakes. I'm not a great flyer and alcohol will only heighten the anxiety. I look around and see some familiar faces at the bar. Jack is yawning while queuing for a pint whereas Tom and Stuart are wide-awake and sinking their lager quickly until it is time to board.

I feel sweat trickling down my arms and my back. I take my seat, clip in my belt and rest my forehead on the back of the seat in front. Campo excitedly sits next to me – he takes it upon himself to try to fix my fears – he does this by telling me tales of turbulence (this doesn't help at all), how many air-miles he has accumulated over the last twenty years (this still doesn't help) and how he's been in a cock pit loads of times (I smile childishly at the word *cock* and recall the humorous scene in *Airplane*) and then I realise that Michael Emenalo is in front of me stuffing his hand luggage into the overhead locker. I try and think of something witty to say but my guts are butterflies and my brain is fluffy. I close my eyes and rest my forehead on the back of Emenalo's seat. I tell myself to grow a pair. Eventually we take off and we're climbing, up-up-and-away. Minutes pass, announcements are made, an air hostess pushes her trolley down and Campo takes a beer and a bacon roll. He tells the hostess that I'll have a bacon roll too. She puts one down, I shake my head, I've got no appetite, I have to choose to think of something else, a place of peace, it will slowly soothe my nerves.

Campo thieves the bacon roll for himself (his plan all along) and I can sense him chuckling at me with every delightful bite. I keep my eyes closed and my head rested for most of the journey.

After what seems like an age we land. As always, once the anxiety has gone, I find myself full of energy to burn. I want to get to the boozer, and quick – we have less than three hours until kick off. We all jump in taxis, Big Chris, Jack and I are in one together and the fat Geordie driver has us in stitches with his quips and tales before dropping us off at the pub where we plan to drink swiftly, meet some friends and pick up some match tickets.

The back bar in this boozer fills up quickly with Chelsea / Rangers supporters, new songs and old are belted out – pint, swig, swallow, pint, swig, swallow, hard and swift. The Baron turns up, we ain't seen each other since Monaco in 2012, we catch up, it's been too long, time goes fast, too fast, the impending 12.45 kick off will shortly interrupt a perfect session, but there are stairs to climb, a game to win, a return flight to catch, *We're Top of the League* gets going, then *sssshhhhh's* ring out louder, the chant dies down, a couple of instantly recognisable Old Bill push their way in. The place is rammed, but they shove through, Fulham's 'finest' pushing their way through the hordes. I concentrate on Goggles – I've not seen him since his little chat with me at Everton. I suddenly remember a Chelsea supporter at Brentford shouting *Harry Potter* at him – and so a chant formulates in my head – *One Harry Potter!* I yell, and the lads join in – *There's Only One Harry Potter, One Harry Potter!* It catches on and rings out, everyone joining in now – his Sergeant laughs but then Goggles's hat gets purposefully knocked off – this brings back memories of the Shed – someone hands it back to him – at least his reinforced spectacles were safe – and I guess I felt a bit of an arse hole for starting the song, but I felt a bit of revenge as well – so what, he could have worse jobs, he'll survive.

I meet Kenny Christmas and pay him for my Southampton tickets. I have a chat with Grinstead John and Sausage Rolls before leaving with Big Chris for SJP. The first half is a blur. Early start, early boozing. I leave on the fortieth minute to get the half-time beers in for everyone. I get to the concourse and find a spot next to a couple of sorts selling plastic bottles of Coors for £4.20. I buy ten and line them up on the shelf behind me and text the lads where I am. Stan teaches us his *He's Not Quite Makelele, Jon Obi* song but it doesn't catch on. Suddenly the second half has started but I'm still on the concourse, a bottle of Coors in each hand, watching it on the TV with a handful of others.

I feel ravenous. I walk over to the food stall and buy a foot long hot dog, it tastes great, and I'm still watching the TV. In the fifty-seventh minute Cisse scores for one nil. I study the replay, JT is well unlucky, he slides in to block the cross and the ricochet could've gone anywhere. I stay where I am watching the TV, the sound of the crowd pouring down the stairs echoes around me, then suddenly it is two nil. I push into the Gents, bladder unloading, I hear Big Chris calling my name, I call back, tell him where I am. I carry on urinating as a bloke to my left pisses and pukes at the same time into the urinal. Then I'm done and moving out the door, skipping down the stairs with Chris. As we leave St. James' Park and venture out into the street, a roar goes up, that's 2-1, we jump into a cab and ask the driver to flick his radio on to the match.

There are seven minutes of injury time. But we have no luck. The full-time whistle goes. We've lost 2-1. Bollocks. The cab driver switches the radio off. We arrive at the airport and leave him a generous tip. We hit the bar – Peroni on tap – the others soon turn up and then even more familiar faced supporters we know take their place for a drink. We are on the last flight of the day to Heathrow and although we lost, I feel in a great place – my anxiety has totally gone. Win, lose or draw it is mates and Chelsea, Italian lager and pretty air hostesses.

On the plane home, Scott sits adjacent to my left. A Geordie lass is sitting next to him. Scott is working his charm. Campo and Stan sit behind the two of them, egging Scott on and asking where the lass is going. She says her name is Rosie and she is flying to Heathrow to connect to Singapore to fly on to Sydney in Australia. The air hostess pushes her trolley down the aisle. She hasn't got any bacon rolls (I'm fuming) but she does give me two cans of Heineken. Scott is trying to deduce what Rosie does for a living. I look at her, studying her clothes, hair and demeanour. I tell myself that she dresses like my Doris and her mates, who are dance teachers. Full of confidence and charm, and eager to put the lads back in their box after my anxieties at Heathrow and the flight out, I ask her with boldness and assurance if she is a dancer. She flicks back her hair and replies with utter annoyance in that wonderfully thick Geordie accent:

"Noooooooooo, pet, I'm a Criminologist!"

Everyone in ear shot collapses in laughter. Old Sherlock here couldn't have been more wrong.

SOUTHAMPTON 1-1 CHELSEA SUNDAY 28TH DECEMBER 2014

Another year ends

My pal Jon and his son Jack are over from Nashville USA. I haven't seen him for a couple of years – not since he flew back to the UK for his brothers wedding. Jon emigrated to Nashville about four years ago, he is back for Christmas and he is taking his 9-year old boy to his first game today. I don't mind admitting that I miss Jon.

We lived in the same town and went to the same church. He was always away playing gigs with his band. On the odd occasion when he was home, we made sure we always went for a few pints. Our local was called The Lamb. We'd wait until our kids were in bed, tell the wives we're meeting up and nip out to the pub. We called it *The Lamb Club.* Our wives mocked us but we didn't care! However, those days are long, long one – but all that matters in this moment is that Jon is here right now – opposite me on a train to Southampton Central. Big Chris has cracked open a Christmas Ale for each of us – and I laugh at Jon as he raises his bottle, grinning at me. The winter sun is shining in through the carriage window and reflecting off his bald scalp. And we're all going to Chelsea away.

Jon explains to us that when he first moved to Nashville and went to a bar to watch a Chelsea game, he smiled at everyone decked from head to toe in their megastore merchandise. They were dripping in blue and white garments. He felt that they looked down their noses at him as he took his place without any colours on – so then he couldn't resist it, so he started to sing *Celery* with his bottle of Bud raised high in the air. The merchandise mob began to nudge each other excitedly and one of them loudly exclaimed: *Hey, he's a real one!* (As in an English Chelsea supporter rather than an American one.)

As the train trundles on, I can't stop checking on Jack. He is so excited. I wonder what is going on inside his mind. He recites players names and numbers, statistics and patterns of play to me. Earlier this morning on my way to the train station to meet them, I popped into the Co-op and filled a bag full of crisps and drinks, chocolate and sandwiches to keep us all going up until kick off – and a *Match of the Day* magazine for Jack to pass the time on the journey.

Smiffy jumps on at Havant. His beard has got bushier and he's got some new Christmas Adidas on. When the Chelsea fans alight at Southampton Central there is a buzz in the air. Hordes of blues scale the steps and a *We all follow the Chelsea* resounds around. I steal a glance at Jack who is wide-eyed with wonder and anticipation, clutching his Dads hand and asking how long it is until kick off.

We get to the boozer and Big Chris tells us to find a table and then he disappears. He comes back with a grin and a tray holding four pints of ale and four jager-bombs. Happy Christmas. I look around. The first person I see is Roger England swaying in the corner and beckoning me over. He tells me that he's been drinking since 2pm yesterday and he hasn't been to bed. He tells me that he has *powered on through* and I tell him he needs a soft drink. I hold up my hand to silence his protest and I dip into my bag of delights. I pull out a ham sandwich. He takes it, rips open the packet, stuffs it into his cake-hole and tells me that it tastes like cardboard. I tell him to drink a pint of water, he says he'll have a Whiskey and Coke. I compromise and buy him a J20. He ignores it, so I drink it instead.

Winston turns up and his two lads run rings round me. They steal my crisps and leg it upstairs. 'Urry Up Dave appears and I introduce him to Jon and Jack. He gives Jack a small pile of fanzines to sell and tells him he can keep any money he makes from his sales. Off Jack goes. He sells them all in a few quick minutes.

I nip outside for a cigarette and a fine young man called Dean comes and says hello. For the last year we've been conversing on Twitter and now we finally meet. We have a pint and a chat, he is a top man, social media isn't so bad at times, I reckon.

Back in the boozer I notice Sausage Rolls is in the OAP corner with True Blue Tel and Grinstead John. I go over and tell them to give it a few seasons and they'll all have walking sticks and free bus passes. I survive a clip round the ear, we all have a Christmas hug instead, we clink glasses, the ale tastes good and is going down a right treat.

I stand and have a look around. I've said it before and I'll say it again. I love the pre-match pub. It is usually the best part of my day. I survey the scene before me. Tape Mix Tim is glowing with the great choices of ale on offer; Smiffy is stroking his beard and chatting to Stock Check Dave; Wickham seems to be necking a pint in one; Dean raises his glass in my direction; Cliff is at a table by the window attentively listening to a friend; Drewsy is checking on a wasted Roger; Seb has his arm around his pretty bit of tottie; Scoots is raising his empty pint glass at Chinese Matt who gives him the finger; Pete is laughing heartily with his pal Steve who always has *Canoville* emblazoned on the back of his retro shirt; Campo is scratching an itch on his neck and is probably thinking about checking my bag to see if there is a bacon roll to thieve; Jon and Jack are posing for a photo taken with a camera phone – they look so happy – Father and Son – Jacks first Chelsea game – this is a special moment.

We get in the ground early so Jack can savour as much as he can. It's been well special watching him taking it all in, it nudges personal memories for me from decades gone by. (The only thing I'll regret is not celebrating with him and Jon. I missed our goal because I had nipped down to the concourse because it was my round.)

It is a few minutes before half-time. As I stand in the queue for refreshments, I remind myself to make this my last drink of the day because I have to work in the morning. Waiting patiently for my turn, my mind drifts off for a moment – the racket of plenty of people hurtling down the stairs to join the queues for booze and food, plus the noise of others starting songs don't register – because I go into a daze contemplating 2014 coming to a close.

The end of another year, another season, another drink, another trip, another queue, another round, another twenty pound note going into a bar till, another article, another fanzine rolled up in the back right pocket of my jeans where it belongs, another morning in the Virtual Waiting Room, another game, another delayed train, another New Year, another resolution, another expectation probably shattered, another dream maybe come true, yes it is the end of another year, now I'm at the front of the queue.

I get served.

And then Eden Hazard equalises.

ROSA PARKS JANUARY 2015 EDITION OF THE CFCUK FANZINE

Go anywhere around the world – anywhere – be it a town, a City, a village – on pavement, on grass, in a car-park, in a back street – even on the Bolivian Salt Flats – produce a football out of a bag and you know what happens, you can guess the rest. A football as a physical object brings people together, no matter what nationality, what background, what language, what beliefs. I've played football in a gypsy camp in Romania, an underground car-park in Buenos Aires, the foot of a mountain in Interlaaken, the stunning beach at Sennen Cove in Cornwall, the gutters of Nairobi, a park in Kiev, a gymnasium near Copenhagen, by a Hotel in Krakow, the harbour in Marseilles, a playground in Nakuru, outside Burger

King in Barcelona, around a pool in Tenerife, my simple green garden lawn in childhood Chessington.

In the years running up to the World Cup in Brazil, thousands of Brazilians took to the streets on various occasions. The people wanted better hospitals, better schools, a more solid infrastructure rather than billions blown on a World Cup. These aren't my words, but the words and feelings of Brazilian people that I have read about. (And we all know how much a Brazilian loves a game of football.)

As the tournament unravelled, I found myself feeling desperate for a David Luiz (Chelsea/PSG) or a Neymar (Barca) or a Marcelo (Real Madrid) to add their voices to those of their compatriots. Hadn't they seen the news? Hadn't they looked out their Hotel windows? Were they oblivious to the cries of a nation – their nation – taking to the streets and getting arrested, tear gassed, bloodied and bruised? Wasn't at least one player going to grow a pair and at least raise the conversation? But then maybe Nike had other ideas (being sponsors of the aforementioned players) and kept their mouths shut as it would be bad for business, I don't know. Some say that the multi-national companies govern the world and have been for years.

Each human life has the most wonderful capability of reaching out to their fellow man. In built in our very system, our very nature, is an instinctive reaction to be kind, compassionate, helpful, selfless – to bring justice in a situation where an injustice has occurred. Thousands, if not millions, wear their poppies with pride. Jesus Christ said: *"There is no greater love than to lay down one's life for one's friends."* Human nature also has an extraordinary capacity to do evil – to abuse, to crush, to slaughter, to dominate, to destroy, to lie, to cheat, to corrupt. Which leads us onto Sepp Blatter and his cruel, corporate backers – driven by greed, drunk on the desire for wealth and control, fixing their own unaccountable system to award a World Cup to Qatar.

The love of money is the root of all evil.

In 2014 an average of one Nepalese migrant worker a day died on the construction sites of Qatar. Leaving their homes to travel there to work to send money back to their families to feed them, these workers are subjected to poor pay, searing heat and deadly site conditions. And what for? WHAT FOR? For a shiny stadium that the 'beautiful' game can be played in. I don't know about you, but I feel both angry and sick. And fairly useless, too. I mean, what can I do about it? Journalists for *The Independent* and *The Guardian* have covered these issues much better than I ever could. Just Google it and you're there to read at will.

FIFA have a multitude of World Cup sponsors. Amongst others, some of the big boys come in the shape of Hyundai, Puma, Adidas, Nike, Emirates, Sony and Coca-Cola. Late in 2014, both Emirates and Sony pulled out of their sponsorship deals with FIFA on ethical and moral grounds. I wrote to them (for what is was worth) to thank them for this decision. As I write this article now, I couldn't find any recent information regarding Puma, but in the back end of 2014 the rumour was they are considering pulling their sponsorship, too. I have also written to Coca-Cola, Hyundai and Adidas, (again, for what it's worth, I mean I just felt that I had to do *something*) to point out what Emirates and Sony have chosen to do and to urge them to do the same. I'm no expert, but I guess that by not advertising on the biggest sporting stage in the world that their profits will no doubt take a hit. Well done Emirates. Well done Sony.

Qatar 2022 is over seven years away. I wonder, as the tournament comes closer, if any current international football players or managers will start to feel the spirit of justice begin to seep under their skin? As the Nepalese death toll rises, as the corruption sinks deeper, as the multi-national disease spreads, will ANY player or manager just start to feel a little bit miffed by all this? Will they start to get a little bit angry? Will they be unable to shake off the desire to speak out? To highlight the injustice of it all? To kick up a storm that PEOPLE ARE DYING IN THE DESERT? Will anyone give FIFA a massive kick in the groin and demand it begins to be governed by righteous and honest people? Will millions of football fans across our planet be able to watch a game of World Cup football without feeling ashamed at the truth that hundreds of slaves perished horribly in Qatar to make the spectacle happen? Maybe International football needs a Rosa Parks. Wherever you are, whoever you may play for or manage, whatever your nationality, when you start shouting from the rooftops to chase the rats out and clean this stinking FIFA ship up, I'll be cheering you on.

If you feel the urge to write a letter, addresses are below:

SONY UK, Technology Centre, Pencoed Technology Park, Pencoed, South Wales, CF35 5HZ.

Emirates UK, 95 Cromwell Road, South Kensington, London, SW7 4DL.

Coca-Cola Great Britain, 1A Wimpole Street, London, W1G 0EA.

Adidas, The Adidas Centre, Pepper Road, Hazel Grove, Stockport, Cheshire, SK7 5SA.

Hyundai Motor UK, PO Box 200, Brockhurst Crescent, Walsall, WS5 4QZ.

JANUARY TRANSFER WINDOW

IN:

Juan Guillermo Cuadrado.
"We'll just call him John Bill Squared."

OUT:

Fernando Torres ("There was something in the air that night, West Ham were shite, Fernando!"); Mark Schwarzer; Andre Schurrle; Ryan Bertrand ("Ryan like a lion in Bayern – Ryan. Lion. Bayern."); Thorgan Hazard.

LOANED OUT:

Alex Davey; Alex Kiwomya; John Swift; Todd Kane; Lewis Baker; Tomas Kalas; Islam Feruz; Marko Marin; Ulises Davila; Nathaniel Chalobah; Joao Rodriguez; Mohammed Salah ("Mo Salah, Salah – Whatever will be will be, you were crap at Shrewsbury, Mo Salah, Salah."); Stipe Perica; Nathan Ake.

PSG V CHELSEA TUESDAY 17TH FEBRUARY 2015

Walts in Malaga

I leave my hotel forty-five minutes before kick off and start to jog to Rafael's. I discovered his bar quite by accident on Sunday when strolling along the beach with my family. We'd walked for about ninety minutes, knowing that once the kids had tired themselves out we'd find a place to stop to have a drink and a bite to eat. Once we were finished, I would ask the proprietor to call us a taxi to take us back to the hotel. So, as it transpired, the place we stopped at was owned by a tall, thin man in his late fifties called Rafael. He looked familiar, but I couldn't place his face. I told myself that it would come to me.

We sat down and I asked for tapas. He said he didn't have any tapas. His English was as bad as my Spanish, but I liked it that way. Even when the food I ordered (which I thought was pork chops) turned out to be a huge plate of fourteen muscles (I counted them), it was all part of the experience. I devoured the lot. A pale, white man in his early seventies sat in the corner with his legs crossed cradling a glass of chilled white wine and smoking a long, thin white cigarette. He wore white trousers. His head adorned with a white fedora hat. He looked like Anthony Hopkins – well, more like the character Hannibal Lector he played, when Lector is residing in Vienna after escaping from prison in the States. I whispered my observation to the Doris. She slapped my leg with a grin, telling me to stop it.

The next day, on my own, I jogged back to Rafael's. It took me half an hour, most of the time I took in the glorious views and thought it was about time I started getting fit again. I was wearing only my shorts, while the locals had their ski jackets and scarves on, giving me disapproving looks for being a half naked Englishman. It was warm for me, freezing for them. After I'd popped my T-shirt back on and ordered my first pint of San Miguel, Rafael placed down a bowl of tapas. (Even though I didn't ask for any, and even though yesterday he said he didn't have any tapas.) The terracotta dish full of carrot, onion, garlic, green olives and gherkins was demolished in uno minuto. I looked up as Hannibal Lector walked in. He sat in the corner and Rafael brought him over a large glass of chilled, white wine. He then bought me out more tapas, this time a portion of large, warm peas decorated with small-diced meat filled the bowl. I asked Rafael if it was chorizo. He said it was jamon. In that moment I realised who he reminded me of. It had been nagging me, (and no, it wasn't that fat oaf Benitez), he reminded me of Tessio from the Godfather – one of Don Corleone's captains. Spitting image.

I was drinking beer with a serial killer and the Mafioso.

By the time I was half way through my third pint, Rafael had placed another bowl of tapas in front of me. This time it was generous lumps of brown sausage slightly sizzling in hot oil. Wonderful. I grabbed a newspaper and pointed at it to show Rafael a specific fixture – PSG versus Chelsea. I tapped my finger on the printed date (tomorrow night) and the kick off time. Rafael smiled and he pointed at the TV saying *yes, yes,* and then I asked for the bill. My three bowls of tapas and three pints of San Miguel came to seven euros and fifty cents. You what? About a fiver! I gave him a tenner and refused the change, telling him I'd see him tomorrow night for PSG v Chelsea.

He shook my hand with a smile saying *yes, yes* again, just like he did before.

So, here I am, match-day, leaving my hotel to jog to Rafael's once again. The hotel is part of a chain called *Holiday World* built into the Benalmedena mountains. I marvelled at the construction – how they've been built into the rock, but then at the same time they are an utter monstrosity – spoiling a wonderful landscape. All at the same time I felt both grateful for my holiday and annoyed at the Hotel ruining the scenery. I jog out of the complex, the pavement bricks under my soles are painted green and yellow. I jog over the road to the edge of the cliff, a simple railing acting as a shoddy barrier to prevent people from an eighty-foot drop down into the sea.

As I jogged along I looked to my left out to the Mediterranean sea and up the coast where Marbella sat far in the distance. Torremolinos was back in the opposite direction – both holiday destinations full of families on their half-term holidays, no doubt most parents are constantly quaffing all-inclusive watered down Dorada lager while displaying fat rolls of English flesh and shouting at their kids. As I watched the waves crash onto the beach I remembered the sandcastle my daughter had built the day before and how my son dodged the waves as they crashed and rolled towards him. I thought about how great it would be to listen to an old local explain to me how the area has changed over the last twenty or so years – I knew the chain of *Holiday World* hotels were built a decade ago. Maybe he would be old enough to recollect The Spanish Civil war. Back in 1937 approximately seven thousand people were killed in only five days during the capture of Malaga. In recent years the area has no doubt gratefully embraced the Euro that came with the holiday-makers, while at the same time shaking their heads at white skin turning pink and the raucous behaviour that inevitably follows after a day on the sauce.

Jogging on, I thought about the last match I attended – the 1-1 draw with City at the Bridge at the end of January. The pre-match boozing session hit me during the game, normally this happens much later, it took me by surprise. I took an age getting myself together and finally coming out the MHU bogs at half-time. I stood by the wall between two gates trying to remember which stairs were the better ones to go up to return to my seat. I was probably swaying in my momentary indecisiveness which caused two stewards to approach me. They demanded to see my ticket. I didn't have it. I was on a spare ST which I'd handed back to my pal after entry. I know what stewards are like. I know how bans are unfairly imposed.... and I knew I was fairly pissed. I weighed it up. Not wanting to get my pal (and his mate whose

ST I had borrowed) in trouble, I simply left and went down the stairs, asking a young bloke in a fluorescent tabard to push the metal bar so I could exit the Bridge and go out into the SW6 air. I decided to walk to West Brompton to clear my head. A bloke well over seven feet tall stopped me and asked for a cigarette. I gave him one. He told his name was Tiny (original), that he'd been on coke for two days without sleeping, that he ran a nightclub in New York and was lost not knowing how to return to his hotel in Imperial Wharf. I took him the one stop on the overground and out he jumped. On I went to Clapham Junction to connect to go home. And that was that.

I shook away thoughts of that game and breathed in the Spanish ocean air. It filled my nose and lungs as I pounded down the hill – the cliff path slowly descending step by step to eventually take me to sea level. I jog harder for fifteen minutes or so until I approach the final corner – Rafael's place just up the road. This was it. Chelsea away to PSG in the European Cup knock out stages – David Luiz, Silva, Cavani, Zlatan and Lavezzi up against John Terry, Matic, Diego Costa, Willian and Azpilicuelta. I was thirsty and expectant – I had that buzz you get before a big game – there was tapas, San Miguel and Sangria coming my way. I felt free, the exercise energising me – the endorphins pushing through my system as I forced myself forwards as I jogged. In this moment I felt relaxed. I embraced contentment. I slow my jog down to a walk. I stretch out then wander up to the bar – then my heart skipped a beat – the shutters are down and the lights are off.

Rafael's was closed. What a load of old flannel.

(Further reading regarding Malaga and The Spanish Civil War: *Dialogue with death* (1937) and *The Invisible Writing* (1953) by Arthur Koestler. Other suggested reading: *Homage to Catalonia* (1938) by George Orwell.)

FOOTBALL, LIFE AND DEATH

Part One – West Ham 0-1 Chelsea. Wednesday 04th March 2015.

West Ham Paul accelerated left and pulled onto the A24 – right hand lane – the engine roaring but not protesting. Trees are flashing past to my left, traffic travelling in the opposite direction speeds to my right, I ease my back into the seat and rest my head – I am tired and deflated, my Aunty getting worse, the cancerous lump in her throat growing quickly, far too quickly. This week I have been in a daze, just like the green leaves blurring as we speed along, my Mum is in pieces – her and my Aunt are twins but my Aunt never married or had kids of her own so she is like my second Mum. She agreed to come and live with me so I could care for her, but then three days later she changed her mind – I was angry and frustrated – ultimately I respected her decision but I was nevertheless left deflated – like an old football in the corner of the garden, or a tennis ball punctured by the chewing of a dog.

I wake up an hour later as Paul pulls into West Ham Nev's driveway. We have a coffee and Zac turns up. Three Irons and me. I stand outside and smoke a cigarette, I dwell on the fact my Aunt has never smoked but has cancer in her lungs, her neck and her throat and as guilt floods me I flick the cigarette into the road and pull myself together, stretch out the niggles in my shoulders and shout at the lads *We're Top of the League!* and they come out of the house singing *Stick Your Blue Flag up your Arse!* and we have a bundle and off we set for Upton Park, all mates together, we just support different teams.

On the tube my chest tightens. Nev was 41 yesterday so he tells me all about his birthday, it takes my mind off my chest as I count the tube stops down. Much later in the evening, I found out all about the tube delays – hundreds of fans didn't make kick off – if I had been stuck like them I would've had to somehow get off the tube. I wouldn't have handled that well at all, a crush of bodies, claustrophobia taking its grip, fear prickling my brain, the tube going nowhere, needing the toilet, sweat and anxiety mixing in the angry atmosphere, gulps of fresh air needed, thinking about my Aunty struggling to breathe, nebulisers and oxygen masks, pegs in the stomach to feed her because she can't swallow, drips in the vein, death creeping closer, stuck on a tube, chest tightening some more, panic attack setting in, thank God that wasn't me.

My Irons' friends and I avoided the tube problems because we'd all left early to go for a curry in Green Street. I swerve any alcohol with my meal, I know it won't heighten my mood, only the opposite will blossom. I eat what I can, I hand Paul some cash on the quiet and tell him to sort Nev out for his birthday present. We plan to meet after the match on the corner by the Chinese where Green Street meets Tudor Road, Smiffy and Big Chris have texted that they're both caught in the traffic issues so I leave the restaurant and make my way towards Upton Park. I wait outside the away end, chatting with those I know, flicking through the fanzine, the end of my toes cold, no sign of my pals, annoyed I didn't put two pairs of socks on, soon it'll be time to get in the ground or I'll miss kick off.

Stock Check Dave arrives half way through the first half. Winston even later. Big Chris gets in right on half-time. The game agitates me because we need that second goal. I lost count of the hundreds of crosses that Downing seemed to whip in down Ivanovic's side, the ref keen to keep his cards in his pockets, we're all used to that now, the final whistles blows, most the away end are singing about winning the league, maybe I needed a few beers to share their enthusiasm – I'm a pessimist, me – I don't join in – I'm in one of those reflective sombre moods where win, lose or draw it doesn't take a priority in some ways – I needed to be lost in the ninety minutes, to take my mind off things, and it did just that, don't get me wrong, I am grateful for the three points of course, but my Aunt is a bad way and no-one can fix it.

Part Two – Chelsea 1-1 Southampton. Sunday 15th March 2015.

I have been in bed for five days. My flu hasn't gone but I'm back to work tomorrow whatever. I don't work, I don't get paid. So I need to get back in. I sit on the train shivering, and I tell myself I'll shiver in my seat at the Bridge too – I would rather be out the house than in bed, I've had enough of my four walls, I've had enough of my duvet, I've had enough of all that shit, I'm proper fed up that I haven't been able to see my Aunty – I couldn't have risked passing this illness on to her so I've kept well away. Smiffy is meeting me in the Fin, it is good to be here, I can't remember the last time I saw these faces in the pub, my head is all bleary, I try and work it out and decide it was before the City game at the end of January – blimey, now it's the middle of March.

I have a cigarette outside The Finny with Sal and Sherman. Smiffy drains his pint and nods at me that it is time to leave. I have to walk slowly. It is the slowest Walk of Glory in the history of Walks of Glories. I feel like shit.

Smiffy and I have brilliant seats in the West, courtesy of Big Beard Bri. Costa put us one up, then Tadic equalised with a penalty. I thought that in the second half we played brilliantly. We put them under so much pressure, but we just couldn't break through. Their keeper Forster was *Man of the Match* and Mike Dean (again) denied us a penalty. Cuadrado came on and lost the ball about three times. Meanwhile, Salah is having the time of his life on loan at Fiorentina. Football, eh? I thought Clyne was quality for them, and maybe the song of the season from their fans: *"St Johnstone's Paint Trophy – You'll Never Win That!"* I have a check. It was only four years ago that they won that, now they're pushing for Europe with a manager that could well be at Tottenham or Man City in two seasons. (Which shows you how much I know, I predicted Koeman would be sacked first.) At full-time my good friend Blanco (a Saints ST holder) sends me a message referring to the second half: *"No-one has battered us this season as much as you.... Hazard is unplayable!"*

After the match, Smiffy and I walk back to the Fin. More slowly than before. I feel shattered. I have a double Jamesons to chase the shivers away and manage to eat half a pizza. On the train on the way home my Mum texts me to say my Aunty has taken a turn for the worse, her breathing isn't great. The train seems to crawl home. An hour felt like a day. I get home, tidy up, and the Doris and I drive to the hospice. Everything goes in slow motion. My Dad is staring vacantly at a painting of a vase of flowers hanging on the corridor wall. My sister rings saying she'll drive down first thing in the morning. A nurse with a clipboard smiles as she walks past me. I push into my Aunt's room.

She smiles when she sees me and I kiss her forehead. Her hair is greasy and smells but I don't care. Seeing her in so much discomfort cuts me deep. Helplessness. I hug her from the side, careful not to knock the equipment to her right. I kneel down and try to hold her hand, but she is uncomfortable, she can't settle. I move to the other side of the bed and sort out the reclining chair for my Mum who will be stopping the night. I suggest to my Dad to go home and get an overnight bag for Mum. I get a blanket out the cupboard for her. My wife is chatting gently, telling Aunty about the kids and stuff, I look into my Aunty's eyes and I can't see hope in them. She has *always* had hope in them, ever since her diagnosis back in 2000. It hits me. It is inevitable. I attempt to blink away the tears but they fall silently anyway. I move over, pushing down the ache in my heart, I tell her I've been to the football, a 1-1 draw, she smiles, I kiss her head again and tell her I'll come and see her after work tomorrow, she nods before one of her growling coughing fits kick in again. It was the last thing I said to her, she passed away at half two in the morning, my Mum holding her hand, twin sisters for sixty-seven years, I thank God for a fitting end, if there is such a thing.

JOHN GEORGE TERRY

Three Memories

1. Kingsmeadow, Kingston-Upon-Thames, Surrey on a Monday night, September 2000.

Smiffy and I filled a minibus full of young people off the Alton Estate in Roehampton to take them to Kingsmeadow where Chelsea reserves were playing Wimbledon reserves. Smiffy's charity REGENERATE, amongst other things, were running two football clubs and two dance clubs (no, neither of us were coaching dance) for 8 to 11s and 12s to 15s. Both season tickets holders at the time, we knew the kids on the estate (which is less than five miles from the Bridge) who supported Chelsea had no chance of affording tickets to go. I knew that occasionally first team players took part in reserve games. I quietly hoped that Zola, Bobby Di Matteo, Wisey or Ferrer would be around. Of course, none of them were, out of the first team only Jon Harley featured and I think Wimbledon won 3-1.

The evening stood out of three reasons. Firstly, once Smiffy had parked the minibus, the doors flew open and a load of over-excited teenagers piled out. Some had Chelsea scarves wrapped around their necks and their excited noise filled the air. Before you could say *Bernard Lambourde* one of them screamed, "There is Claudio fucking Ranieri!", and they all legged it across the car-park. By the time I'd undone my selt-belt, got out the door and caught up with them they were posing for photographs and offering him M&Ms. I smiled awkwardly and uncomfortably at the Chelsea employee accompanying Mr Ranieri (possibly Gary Staker?) but there was no need. In broken English the new Chelsea manager welcomed them, he embraced them and posed for some photos. I looked around for Smiffy wondering where he'd got to – sure enough he came ambling up with a big grin on his face holding a bag of chips from the refreshment van. He shook hands with our new manager and offered him a chip. Claudio gratefully tucked in. It was all rather bizarre, but absolutely brilliant.

Secondly, the next 'highlight' of the evening involved Graham Rix. He was present in a scruffy jacket with a note book and pen. I had no idea who he was scouting for, but he became Portsmouth manager soon after. I had to restrain a 13 year old lad called Matt with ADHD, (Attention Deficit Hyperactive Disorder) who threatened to smash up Rix and then put in all the windows in his motor after he had told Matt in no uncertain terms to, "go away, you annoying little kid," after Matt asked for a photo and an autograph. Mr Rix had a lot to learn from Mr Ranieri and quite frankly was lucky Matt didn't boot him right in his Gentleman's Sausage before I could drag him away (in angry tears, I might add) from the grumpy old has been.

Thirdly, upon leaving, the young people were dragging their heels across the car park back to the minibus when one of them spotted John Terry. Once again, they all legged it across the car park and piled straight up to him. If I remember rightly he had two dogs with him, and both were stroked and petted and probably fed the odd melted M&M from a messy pocket. I groaned a little inside when Kirsty asked if he had a girlfriend and then if he had any free tickets, but JT took it in his stride. He chatted with them all and I shook his hand and thanked him before ushering all the teenagers back into the minibus. Matt's tears had gone and his wide, cheeky beam had returned. As for JT (who was maybe checking that his wallet hadn't been lifted), well it was to be nearly fourteen years until I got the chance to shake his hand again, this time just the two of us.

2. Ewood Park, Blackburn, Wednesday 02nd February 2005.

If we won at Ewood, Chelsea would be eleven points clear at the top. What a position to be in. Could we dream of winning the league? Pessimism was still prevalent in most of our support – me included! In our previous match we'd beaten Pompey 1-0 at The Bridge and exactly a week before thousands had travelled to Old Trafford where we beat United 2-1 to reach the final of the League Cup where we'd play Liverpool at the Millennium Stadium. What a time to be a Chelsea supporter.

The fact is, we beat Rovers 1-0 thanks to an Robben goal in the fifth minute. But there was so much more to this game than the three points. Alex Ferguson, in truth, had played a psychological blinder (he hoped) in stirring the pot, citing our up coming fixtures against Rovers, City and then Everton would be pivotal because teams from the North West of England would raise their games and be tough to beat.

Blackburn Rovers were brutal on that Wednesday evening. Referee Uriah Rennie was completely out-of-his-depth (when wasn't he) and in truth Dickov, Matteo and Mokoena should all have been sent off. The latter wasn't even booked, despite putting Robben out the game, injuring him with a disgusting challenge. Chelsea fan and ex Chelsea player Mark Hughes lost thousands of friends that night. Sparky had clearly sent his players out to do one on us. The weak referee contributed to the vicious performance of Rovers players such as Savage, Todd and Nelsen. Our away end was going absolutely ballistic in anger at what was unfolding before us, but the euphoria to follow saw celebrations that we're completely unique to both the players and the travelling support – I mean, we'd never been eleven points clear before, had we?!

On sixty minutes Rovers were awarded a penalty. A post-match report summarised: *"On the hour mark the hosts got the perfect opportunity to level, referee Uriah Rennie pointing to the spot after Ferreira was adjudged to have clipped Savage's legs in the box. But Cech was more than equal to Dickov's low spot-kick, sprawling away to get his giant left hand in the way...."* Emotion in the away end swung from rage to elation. It was a soft penalty. We all knew it. Everyone knew it. We were being stitched up. Programmes were angrily flung through the air on to the pitch. It wasn't like we'd blown it, we were being done. I waited for the net to bulge to signal Blackburn's equalizer. It never came. IT NEVER CAME! Big Pete had saved it! And then he blocked the follow up! Later we learned that Dickov should have been sent off for leaving his foot in on our keeper. It was one of those celebratory moments when you fall into the row in front, clutching the mates beside you (in this case, Tall Paul and Smiffy) and all the air went out of our opponents and Chelsea won, and we were eleven beautiful points clear.

What happened next has gone down in Chelsea folklore. Now, we've all got used to JT thumping his chest and punching his fists in celebration. It is his signature. The more pumped up he is, the bigger his eyes widen, the more his biceps bulge and the veins in his neck jut out to bursting point. But this was like he'd just emerged victorious as a gladiator in the coliseum. Led by JT, the players threw their shirts in the crowd, the stewards pushed supporters back trying to get on the pitch, I was so buzzing I would walk home for all I cared. Describing this moment being a pivotal occasion for Chelsea Football Club was a massive understatement.

At least twice this season I've heard people describing recent games as our *'Blackburn 2005'* moment – Stoke away at Christmas and QPR away only last week spring to mind. Personally, I'm not having that. I know what they mean in terms of describing Chelsea's resilience, spirit, courage and determination – and our opponents take out Hazard like they'd foul Robben – plus how refs seem to consistently refuse to book or send off opposition players for brutal treatment. But that's where the comparisons end for me. That night at Ewood, Chelsea had arrived. Bubbles of pessimism burst with every fist pump from our Captain. Yes, John George Terry epitomised this. We were eleven points clear. We'd broken all that Fergie, Wenger, refs and opponents could throw at us. We fucking believed. Just like a team that's gonna win the Football League, we shall not be moved.

The season ended like this: P38 W29 D8 L1 GD+57 PTS 95. Our Captain John Terry won the Player of the Month award in January, was the PFA Players Player of the Year and in the PFA Team of the Year. So, was I at Bolton when the league was finally sealed? No. I was out on a boat on the Whitsunday Islands in Australia. After the match at Ewood I flew to Brisbane, also missing our League Cup win versus Liverpool. As a true Chelsea pessimist, I decided in the summer of 2004 that Jose would need a season to over-take (if at all) Fergie's United and Wenger's Arsenal, so I booked a four month trip away with the Doris. What a monumental plonker.

3. Cobham High Street, Surrey, August 2014.

My Doris hadn't been out of bed for six weeks after an operation. She had another six weeks to go before she could return to work. We went to Cobham to stay for a night at her parents, a different four walls for her to look at, a break from her own bedroom, her spirits needing to be lifted. It was a nice afternoon, so we went down to Carluccio's for a coffee. Well, if the truth be told, we both ended up having a couple of cocktails. I was facing the window. If I had sat in the other chair, I never would have seen him. I looked up and JT walked past. Fuelled by two Lemon Spriztes (three parts sparkling Limonata, two parts Limoncello, one part Proscecco) I legged it out the shop and chased after him. I felt like a bit of a lemon if truth be told, and couldn't think of anything to say. I mean, I can sing about him before, during and after a match, but when it came to shaking his hand my mouth went dry and my normal fat gob was well and truly shut. I can stand on the back of my seat, lean on my pals for balance and start chants in pubs and on concourses and in grounds home, away and in Europe – but right here on Cobham High Street my brain had gone all foggy. He asked what I was doing and I said me and the wife were having a drink, and that she was recovering from an operation. John wished her all the best. And that was pretty much it. We went our separate ways. I was absolutely buzzing but frustrated at the same time that I couldn't think of anything of significance to say.

Since bumping into JT at Kingsmeadow, it has been a crazy ride. Back in 2000/01 he made 23 starts and we voted him Chelsea's Player of the Year. On 05th December 2001, JT was captain of Chelsea for the first time, in a League game against Charlton. His name has been sung name all over the world – if you include Japan. He has lifted trophies. He has been roared on after blocking tackles time and time again. Thousands have shaken jubilant fists back at him in victory after he has come over to our travelling section to celebrate hard fought wins. But the most brilliant thing that I love JT for the most, more than all of these things mentioned, is that he agrees with us all that Rafa Benitez is a right prick.

Cheers for everything, John George Terry.

CHELSEA 1-0 MANCHESTER UNITED
SATURDAY 18TH APRIL 2015

We shall not be moved

I take mini Walts, aged six, to his mate's house and I jump in a taxi to the train station. To say I'm buzzing about today is an understatement. It doesn't matter how old I get, I'm a like a kid, and the train journey will drag, I just want to get to the boozer to meet everyone.

The taxi driver tells me that a rumour is going around that someone recently jumped at Aldrington, near Hove, so the trains to Brighton were all cancelled. I check it out once I get to the station. He was correct. No trains were running on this railway line.

I consider my options while leaning against the station wall and smoking a cigarette. Whatever happened in that person's life to push them to the edge must've been truly frightening. I wonder if it was a man or a woman, young or old. Maybe it was a build up of brutal experiences happening day after day, year after year until they could take no more, or may be it was a instant thing like the death of a friend, a child, a spouse that had made them decide to end it all. I picture someone launching themselves off a platform into a speeding train. I shudder, shake the image away, look up to the sky and pull on my cigarette.

Suddenly I become aware of two Palace fans that are cursing their bad luck and fumbling for their phones to get on to National Rail Enquiries. I recognise one lad from the church I go to – Aaron – but we'd rarely spoken. I tell them what I'd heard and I suggest to them that we could get an alternative train line to the Capital – there is an adjacent line that bypasses Hove and Brighton and goes through Billingshurst and Pulborough and then to Haywards Heath. I float the idea of sharing a cab to either Haywards Heath or Horsham, and hop on a train to London that way. However, Aaron's pal tells me his car is parked around the corner, so we hop in, drive to nearby Barnham, a train turns up a few minutes later, and that was that.

We sit around a table and Aaron offers me one of his cans out of his blue carrier bag. We talk about all kinds of football related stuff, including the League Cup game between Palace and Chelsea in the early nineties (I think 1992 but I'm probably wrong) when the rain was so torrential and the pitch so soggy, a Chelsea 'goal' never happened because the ball got stuck in the mud to prevent in from crossing the line. And Palace won.

As the train pulls into East Croydon we wish each other *good luck* and off they go. *Thornton Heath; The Railway Telegraph; Clifton Arms; Selhurst Park; Glad All Over; Malcolm Allison's fedora; A young, raw Ian Wright; Terry Venables with a neat side-parting; David Hopkin in 1997 at Wembley; Paul Canoville's debut in 1982; A ball stuck in the mud.* I rub my hands on my jeans and look out the window as the train accelerates towards Clapham Junction – no matter how much I want it to, I cannot make it travel any faster. I feel thirsty. My can is long gone.

I'm right up at the doors when the train pulls into Clapham. The *OPEN* button flashes its yellow lights and I push it and step off. On the platform the multitudes manoeuvre one way or the other, doing a dance almost as people step aside, step forward off the train or step forward on to it – a guards whistle blows, I cruise down the steps and onto the concourse. I'm walking quickly, overtaking those slower than me and ducking my shoulder in so I don't bump those coming in the opposite direction, I go to the end of the station and turn right before I reach the ticket machines. Then I turn right to exit and trot up the stairs and on to the West Brompton bound overground train, perfect timing.

I take a seat and within a minute the train moves. As it rattles towards Imperial Wharf I look out the window, as always, and study the Thames. It takes my mind off feeling thirsty. I become aware that I'm tapping my feet. I repeat the same routine. I get up and stand by the doors as the train begins to slow. I ignore a man with his arm raised high, his hand holding the orange rail above his head for balance. I don't look at him, but I can smell him, his whiff is stale and unwelcome, I long for the flashing, yellow buttons to appear so I can press *OPEN* and escape the overbearing odour.

It's a wind up at West Brompton station. They don't open the gate like they used to, so I've got to go into the station, cross above the underground lines then queue to exit into the street opposite Earls Court. But once I'm out, it's good. Ironically, now I'm here I don't even rush, really. I put my hand into the breast pocket on my shirt and pull a cigarette out of the packet and walk towards Finborough Road, the cemetery to my right, buses, cars, motorbikes and taxis vying for precious space in the Saturday lunchtime traffic.

I step into the Finny and wish Roger England a *Happy Birthday* – his Mum nods towards the bar and points at a variety of photos of her son adorning the tiles on the wall. I choose my drink carefully – a pint of dark ale brewed in Ledbury – I don't stay long because once Jim and Smiffy drain their glasses we all leave to walk to the stall to sign up to the Qatar protest. (It goes without saying that Jim loved the *Walk of Glory* – especially the can of G&T that I pressed into his palm as we turned down Seagrave Road.)

Since January, (when I had last written about Qatar), over 1400 workers have now perished constructing World Cup Stadia for the 2022 tournament. And that still does not sit right with me. I felt I had to respond, to do something, to at least put my head on the pillow at night knowing I added my voice to a growing number of angry, frustrated and bewildered voices at this slavery and injustice. We met up with Sausage and AJ and Terri and joined our voices to the gathering cause – one lit candle might not be too bright, but put in next to a hundred others and it becomes harder to ignore. Momentum for change has to start somewhere.

Once we'd been at the stall, we turned in the opposite direction with Stamford Bridge behind us and headed for Dawes Road. The road sign always reminds me of a chapter in *Among the Thugs* when Chelsea and United have a massive tear up. The chapter is simply called *Dawes Road, Fulham.* One of the bouncers outside holds the door of The Mitre open for us, and in we stride. I look around. The pub has undergone a significant refurbish since I was last in here. It turns out the refurbishment only happened last week! Here we meet Taxi Alan, Den and young Zac. We had a great catch up and finally Big Chris arrived.

We all pile outside for a cigarette and embraced Champagne Les, Vastly Intelligent Keef and Tax Dodging Tommy in the beer garden. We then found out (identical to what the Cock did several years ago), that once the refurbishment was done, the management decreed that no-one wearing football colours was allowed in the pub. Champagne Les popped his cork – he was fuming, and rightly so. He zipped his jacket up, respectfully remonstrated with a bouncer to voice his complaints before returning to his Guinness and into the bosom of his pal Keef to moan about how poorly SW6 pubs can treat their paying customers.

I look around the beer garden. I see a few faces that I

haven't seen for a while. In fact, I think I only met them once. I work it out. Amazingly, it will only be a few days and then it will be exactly three years since I briefly saw them. I was in Barca with Smiffy the night before *that game* in the Nou Camp having a drink with Cathy, when these lads, all older than me, turned up and they all knew each other and were chatting to Cathy. One of them had an orange Lacoste polo on. Every was singing *Easy Jet, Easy Jet, Easy Jet* at him. So, I go over to him now. He looks at me like he doesn't know me (he doesn't) but when I explain how I remember him, he cracks up laughing. His mates recall the story, too, and then he ducks his head towards me grinning and admits quietly that *I haven't worn that fucking top since!* Brilliant.

I've had plenty to say in the past about the atmosphere at Stamford Bridge, but I have no complaints this time. The place was absolutely bouncing. I love it when it is like that. Everyone all up for it, playing our great rivals, the title closing in! I must admit I felt Rooney and Herrera really influenced the game, I was impressed with them both – same for Luke Shaw. But, unusual for me, I felt optimistic and positive throughout – though obviously I had no confidence in the ref Mike Dean, but thankfully he did his job well. At full time no-one around me was in a rush to leave – this was it – belief and relief entwined as the anthems belted out regarding winning the league and for the first time this season I joined in too. As I exited the MHL the whole crowd was singing *We Shall Not be Moved* and it continued into the Fulham Road. In hindsight, I should have shimmied up a lamp post or climbed on the bus shelter to watch the blues supporters singing triumphantly into the early evening air as they marched towards the tube or further on towards North End Road. What a sight that would have been.

I returned to the Fin to drink with the hordes. Everyone was in party mode. I pushed my way through to the far end of the pub and leant my elbows on the bar. I was in no rush to get served. I was happy to contemplate. So, if we beat Arsenal on Sunday and Leicester the Wednesday after, I think that made us Champions. Were we? Were we really? Was this really happening? Or, if we draw with Arsenal (as I, and many others expect), then beat Leicester, we have two home games (against Palace then Liverpool) to clinch it. The chatter of those squashed in around me were working out the possibilities, too. Galvanised by beating United, the euphoria in the pub was tangible, there was no way with Jose in charge and JT and Eden playing the football of their life were Chelsea going to throw this away. I was smiling happily to myself. I waved at Tape Mix Tim opposite me at the other side of the bar. Jeff asked me what I was drinking, and I ordered a pint of

Mad Goose....

....And then I happened to look up and notice, through the window, at a coach full of United supporters appear and stop right outside! The driver slowed due to a red light and braked to a halt right next to a throng of jubilant Chelsea drinking in the cool evening air.

I nearly choked on my pint with laughter watching the fuming, red-faced Mancs launch out of their seats and go right up against the coach windows gesticulating with wild fury while the Chelsea boys mocked them with laughter and *wanker* signs. Inside the coach, one Manc climbed on his seat and forced open the 'sun-roof' (it was on restrictive hinges) and the only things he could find to Frisbee out were plastic trays and cutlery from the meals they'd recently consumed. When the lights went green the coach driver accelerated and everyone laughed and mocked the Mancs some more as they went out of sight towards Earls Court as thin, plastic trays drifted pathetically down out of the splendid SW6 sky.
The party mode continued – even the Makelele Macarena (with actions) was performed by Big Chris and Charley – and when Marmite Pete climbed on to the roof of a white van to start singing I looked at the time and saw it was nearing half past nine. Big Chris and I near enough had a three hour journey home. I

watched him singing. He was definitely swaying a little. I grabbed him by the arm, gave him my forgotten hot dog (still in the wrapping) that had been in my pocket since half-time and we headed for West Brompton. Once on our connecting train from Clapham, I groaned a little because the carriages were packed with Gooners returning from their FA Cup semi at Wembley, but the lads I was with were top draw. The oldest member of the group, 83 years old, bemoaned the move from Highbury to the Emirates, citing the club never stuck to their promise of relocating supporters together so those they had been sitting around for years at the old ground could do so at the new.

I listening with empathy and sadness for his situation. All these years on and he was still feeling robbed by it all. One lad had paid £105 (face value) for his ticket which, in my opinion, is a disgrace. When I went to get off the train at my stop I wished them luck in the cup, (it felt like the polite thing to do) and they congratulated Chelsea on the fact they'd be winning the league. As I stepped off the carriage I gave them a rendition of *We Shall not be Moved!*

For the first time this season, I believe. Come on, Chelsea!

AND LEICESTER 1-3 CHELSEA WEDNESDAY 29TH APRIL 2015

One hand on the trophy

Five years I've lived where I live, and I've met some good people. And some right plonkers. Leicester Chris is one of the good guys. I first met him around the poker table down the local, it never takes long after an introduction to get on to the subject of football.

Chris drives to every Leicester game – home or away – and after we first met we talked about the key games between our clubs over recent years. In February 1997 Chelsea went up to Filbert Street in the fifth round of the FA Cup. Chris reels off key members of the Leicester squad managed by Martin O'Neill – Kasey Keller, Spencer Prior, Gary Walsh, Garry Parker, Ian Marshall, Steve Claridge. I watched the game on the TV. I can recall Chelsea fans celebrating in the Leicester end, Jimmy Hill having a moan about the scuffles that followed, Frank Sinclair hoofing a ball so high it cleared the stand and bounced in the road and Gianfranco Zola receiving boos from the home crowd – it was only a few days since his winning goal for Italy saw off England at Wembley in a World Cup Qualifier. The only other Chelsea player on the Wembley pitch that night was Roberto Di Matteo. Interesting to note that a certain Lazio striker called Pierluigi "Gigi" Casiraghi ran himself into the ground for his country that night.

To counter Chris, I reel off key members of our squad that season. Ruudi as our player-manager, old battle axe Mark Hughes, Steve Clarke, Dan Petrescu, Wisey our captain playing alongside the heroic Bobby Di Matteo – then I wink at Chris and tell him Frank LeBoeuf loved scoring penalties and Chris pulls a face and tells me never to mention Erland Johnsen and I say that I don't have to, because he just has.

I explain to Chris what an incredible season that was for me and for Chelsea. I turned 21 years of age in June 1996, and my parents upgraded my membership to a season ticket for my birthday. I had moved out at

19 when they relocated to the Midlands – I was in a low paid job – I covered my rent and bills every month but didn't have much left for the football. (In fact, I only went away once that season – a 2-0 loss to Forest.) Now I had a season ticket. My wooden seat was right above the benches in the West Stand. Every game I looked mournfully to my right at the demolished Shed end and felt cheated that a packed terrace wasn't falling in jubilation as the goals went in – for example, Zola twisting up Julian Dicks or when Vialli scored his first for the Club against Coventry City. He buried the ball past Steve Ogrizovic and wheeled away in delight, *Coors* on his chest, Diadora boots on his feet and Chelsea sweatbands on his wrists.

The 96/97 season finished on a high for both teams. Leicester won the League Cup and Chelsea won the FA Cup. We both beat Middlesbrough in our respective finals. Over the years I have heard Leicester fans bitterly complain more at Erland Johnsen winning a penalty for his team in that fifth round replay than I have heard them talk about the fact they won the League Cup two months later! Their final with Middlesbrough went to a replay. Steve Claridge got the winner in extra-time. The replay was staged at Hillsborough. Just the mention of that stadium conjures memories of another Leicester v Chelsea match.

On 15th April 1989, Chelsea played at Filbert Street and lost two nil. A point would have seen Chelsea promoted from the Second Division. I wasn't at the game, but my friends Champagne Les and Vastly Intelligent Keef were. Over the many years drinking with Les and Keef pre-match, I can only recall them talking about this game once before. Some people say 10,000 Chelsea fans had gone up that day. It was kicking off all over the place. Others say that they reckon the ref that day was as bent as can be. But all these things are partly irrelevant, for now. Champagne Les only spoke about the fact that on that day at Filbert Street he truly feared for people's lives as they were herded and crushed. On the way back to the car he said that it was only a matter of time before people would die from being crushed at the football. Once in the car, he flicked on the radio to hear that it had already just happened – seventy miles away in Sheffield at Hillsborough.

It was New Years Eve. 2012 was soon to evolve into 2013. Leicester were flying in the Championship, pushing for promotion to the Premiership. In the pub, I told Leicester Chris we'd be meeting in the league once again next season. Chris said there was a long way to go. As January rolled into February, Leicester were second in the league. Chris still said there was a long way to go. He was right. They only won two of their following sixteen games! What subsequently happened sums up the pain and glory of supporting a football team. On the last day of the season, they had to beat fierce rivals Forest (who also needed a win for a play-off place) and hope Bolton did not win. Bolton drew. Chris said the scenes in the away end were up their with the best ever when a late winner from Anthony Knockaert meant Leicester beat Forest 3-2 to clinch the final play-off spot on goal difference!

However, the pain was to follow. They lost the semi-final at Vicarage Road. Four minutes into injury time Leicester won a penalty. Up stepped Anthony Knockaert. If he scores, they're in the final. The keeper saved the penalty, then amazingly blocked the rebound, the ball was cleared and Watford broke away and scored. Just like that. Zola, who was Watford's manager, fell over celebrating – he was taking Watford to Wembley. Incredible. A day or two after, I pushed into the pub and saw Leicester Chris in the corner with a mate. I took him over a pint, put it down in front of him, patted his shoulder and off I went. Luckily for him, the Foxes were promoted the following season. We both waited in anticipation, as so many of us all do, for the 2014/15 fixture list to come out to see when we would meet. And it was bad news.

My Doris is more than happy for me to go to the football. She knows I love it, and it gets me out of her hair for a day. However, when it comes to her birthday, I have to pull out all the stops. For half a decade, since we've known each other, Leicester Chris and I have been waiting to go to the New Filbert Street together, and would you believe, our fixture is on my Doris's birthday. It wasn't even negotiable. What a load of old flannel.

But then, a few months later, I noticed something.

Nine days before Christmas we beat Derby 3-1 away in the League Cup quarter-finals. I studied the fixture list to look for the date of the Final. It was the Doris's birthday. Which meant that if Chelsea got to the final, our away match with Leicester would be rearranged. Which was exactly what happened. I didn't go to Wembley in February, but I was going to Leicester in April. And the scene was set. Chelsea had drawn with Arsenal 0-0 at the Emirates. Arsenal were absolutely fuming that we 'played for a draw' despite the fact we should have had two penalties plus their keeper should've been sent off for an assault on Oscar. Their bitterness made our point even sweeter – we'd avoided defeat and thus were two wins away from winning the league.

Leicester Chris said he'd pick me up after lunch. My

morning absolutely dragged. I couldn't sit still. Daft, I know. When he eventually turned up and I got in the car, he confirmed we were going A24, M25, M1. Then he waggled his finger at me and said:

–I've got three rules, Walts.

–This sounds ominous, I said.

–Rule one – no smoking in the car.

–Goes without saying, Chris.

–Rule two – we split the petrol.

–Nah, bollocks – you're driving. I get all the petrol.

–It's non-negotiable.

–Don't be a doughnut, I'll pay for the lot.

–My car, my rules.

–I'm not going to argue with you....

–That's settled then, he said, cutting me off.

–And rule number three?

–You're not going to like it.

–Go on....

–Because it's a mid-week game, we leave on eighty minutes, mate.

My heart sank. What if it's nil-nil? And then in the 89th minute, Petr Cech comes up for a corner and buries the winner? And we storm the pitch in a rush of euphoria? I'll miss it. All kinds of scenarios were going around my head. Ultimately I knew I had to respect Chris's decision.

–Okay mate, I said.

He could hear the dejection in my voice, even though I tried to hide it.

–Thing is, if we leave on full-time, it takes me an hour just to get to the motorway. I'm not as young as I used to be. I've got a business to run, he explained, momentarily taking his hands off the steering wheel and shrugging his shoulders and holding his palms face up.

–I know, I know mate. It's fine, I whimpered, fumbling in my pocket for my phone to distract myself with Twitter.

As we headed towards the M25, I told myself that it didn't matter. Mentally, I listed off all the positives. There were plenty. I told myself that however the game panned out on the pitch from the eightieth minute was out of my control. I couldn't dictate what happened on the pitch, but then I could be a part of the crowd that dictates what happens in the stands that inspires our players on the pitch. For instance, if the away following was belting out *Chelsea Chelsea Chelsea* from the eightieth minute until the final whistle, I wouldn't be there taking part, on my seat, losing my voice, driving the players on.

What will be, will be.

By the time we get to the M1, the heavens open and I fall asleep.

Once we've parked up in Leicester I find my way to the pub where Garry is boozing and we have a couple of pints and a burger and chips before walking to the ground. The rain has ceased, thankfully, and as Garry goes in I take a stroll round the stadium to meet my friends Ann and Olly that I've arranged to see at 7pm. I seem to have a few pals who support Leicester. It's good to catch up. The rain has long gone and the sun is coming out.

I re-trace my steps towards the away end, a crowd has gathered and not many are making their way through the turnstiles. One of D's famous Chelsea coaches has recently turfed out its occupants, and to say they are well oiled is an understatement. I catch up with a couple of familiar faces and then I spot No Beans Kenny. I haven't seen him since Everton away. He's got dodgy knees and one of his trouser legs is caught on a bandage that seems to run from his ankle up to his thigh. I crouch down and sort it out for him and before he goes I take a selfie with him so I can send it to The Baron to remind him of our trip to Monaco. We were in a boozer and Kenny kept sending back his food (three times, I think) because they kept putting Baked Beans on his plate, and he most certainly wanted no beans with his breakfast.

I follow No Beans Kenny into the ground. The concourse is bouncing. I spot Gaz at the front of the bar and he gets me a lager in. Perfect timing. Famous appears. Josh is wearing a magic hat. Slough Jon has his arms around two of his pals. I take the moment in, enjoying it, and I try and remember the last away end that was as drunk as this one. Famous reckons Man City in the FA Cup when it was a Saturday five-thirty. I push my way into the toilets and everyone is both pissed and pissing – and singing their hearts out.

As usual, the whole away end is standing. My seat (not that I sat in it) was right on the back row and right in the middle. Perfect. I look along the row and I see another Kenny – this young rascal is Kenny Christmas – you see, just like Santa, he sorted out my ticket for today. I blow him a kiss and I get a wave and a smile back. With the rain clouds dispersed and the sun going down, the sky-line is beautiful. However, the first half is awful. Drogba was doing his best impression of Emile Heskey on a bad day. Much to my delight, *One Erland Johnsen* gets a brilliant airing and then the Foxes take a deserved lead. We've got to liven ourselves up. Jose will put a rocket up them at half-time. I think to myself that it suddenly seems daft now singing all those songs about winning the league after our win against United and point against Arsenal. We've been terrible. Plus, now I'm faced with a quandary. It is decision time – do I relieve my bladder again now, or wait until maybe the 78th minute and go on my way out, just before I meet Chris for the drive home? I decide to stick it out.

Within three minutes of the re-start Drogba equalises. What was the fuss about? The away end erupts, belief returns and time ticks on. As the Americans say, I need to take a leak. I'm fuming with myself. I should've gone at half-time. This could be a nightmare scenario. I could urinate now, then leave a little after eighty minutes and sprint to the meeting place. That'll work. My bladder is telling my brain that it is full up. Sixty minutes turns into sixty-five. Sixty-five turns into seventy – I'm desperate now so I decide to go for a piss. I leg it down the yellow steps, down the spiral stairs, push into the bogs and give it all I've got. I finish up, sprint back up the stairs, come out onto the yellow steps and John Terry sticks it in for 2-1. Absolutely fucking brilliant.

Arms and legs are everywhere. I'm still on the yellow steps. Everyone is going potty. I hear my name shouted and my breath is squeezed out of me as Mad Gray grabs me in an embrace and Bearded Bri comes round the other side and we celebrate together. I notice that Mad Gray has his mustard yellow Adidas on. I might be nowhere near my seat, but somehow I've ended up with pals. I stay here for the rest of the match.

I look to my left and see the BFG and Liz, Mr Away and Terrence. I look to my right and there's Beefy with his top off, pissed up and swinging his shirt around his head. I shout his name but he can't hear me. *Boring Boring Chelsea* rings out over and over again. And then Ramires goes and sticks one in the top corner. Fucking pandemonium. I jump on the barrier behind the SKY cameraman and Bri joins me. We've basically done it. One hand on the trophy. Three more points and it's ours. And that won't be a problem. We've wrapped it up. Jack appears out of nowhere so I jump off the barrier into him for a celebratory embrace – he then goes to jump up on the barrier himself, except he climbs on the front section in front of the cameraman which means it is basically a drop down onto the concrete below. I pull him off the barrier before he stacks it down below. Then I realise the time. So I leg it.

Down the yellow steps I go and then the spiral staircase. A old steward pushes down on the metal handle and pushes opens the door for me. I say *thanks* and I feel like giving him a hug, I'm laughing and I'm buzzing, no other Chelsea fan has left the ground, just me. As I jog out into the street, the Willian song goes up – he's obviously being subbed off. I jog quickly in the direction of the meeting place where Leicester Chris awaits me as the Chelsea choir sings *He Hates Tottenham* loud and proud.

You couldn't make it up.

It's all worked out rather perfectly.
Back cover photo, Leicester away, by @xLizziDx

CHELSEA 1-0 PALACE
SUNDAY 03RD MAY 2015

Champions!

Big Chris is at Clapham Junction, platform two, grinning at me as I walk towards him. This will be the last time we do this for weeks, maybe months. It will be our last game of the season, even though we still have to play Liverpool, WBA and Sunderland, neither of us will be going again. He is off to New Zealand for the whole summer, so it could be September before we meet like this once more. September! It doesn't bear thinking about. As he greets me, he puts a twenty pound note in my hand. He tells me it's for my train fare. Things have been a bit tight this month, he knows that and he knows why. What goes around, comes around. We've been through a lot since we first met – Chelsea bound us together – as it does for so many – and now it's mental because we were best men for each other when we got married, both moved around a bit, and now my kids are mates with his kids – I really have to pinch myself sometimes – I count my blessings, I have to, if I don't then life feels tougher – my battle isn't your battle, and your battle isn't mine – but I'm lucky to have mates like him and Smiffy – and I get all sentimental like that when I'm having a drink and reflecting on things – it's not just Chelsea supporters either – Seagull Si and West Ham pals Nev and Paul are just as important to me, too.

In the Fin I finally get to meet @cliveoconnell author of the splendid *'Driver on the Wing'* articles published online by the Chelsea Supporter's Group. He introduces me to his lovely daughter Louisa which makes me wonder why some of the single lads like Tape Mix Tim aren't over here offering to take her out for lunch. Smiffy and Big Chris are ticket-less, so are staying in the pub to watch it, so the wonderful Terri accompanies me on the Walk of Glory. As we stroll down Seagrave Road I point to my left where they're building flats in the car park – I tell her I always think of Munich because that car park is where my coach left from. Then I point to my right at the specific place where the lads stop for a slash to empty the bladder, and she hits me and scolds me as usual, and make our way to the stall and then of course to Stamford Bridge.

Today Stock Check Dave is my ticket fairy, and as I wait for him by the statue of Peter Osgood I take a deep breath and people watch. Tourists have their photos taken outside the West Stand entrance. Dads and Mums take pictures of their kids leaning against the wall. Lads in groups clench fists and sing about winning the league. Geezers of all ages that I recognise from past seasons both recent and prehistoric make their way past me. Some fans touch the statue before moving on. Stock Check Dave turns up and we queue at the turnstiles. We push in. I savour it. I'm not gonna be here for a while. Inside the lager flows. Same old. Dave tells me Winston is running late, caught in traffic after taking his boys to their Sunday morning game.

It's a tight match. To be honest I expected the opposite. I thought we'd come out and smash them all over the shop. And then a miracle happened. We were awarded a penalty. I have probably sat with Stock Check and Wee Willie Winston a good ten times in their seats in the MHL, and the chap in front is a quirky character. As soon as we were awarded a penalty he turned around, folded his arms and looked at me.

– Can’t you watch? I ask.

– No, he replies.

–Why ever not? I grin, somewhat intrigued.

–I ain't watched a penalty since Dixon missed two against Portsmouth in 83/84. He says, and looks to the floor, expecting the worst.

(It occurred to me afterwards that the next time I see him, I'll ask him about Munich. I mean, I know he would've looked at the floor for all of Chelsea's penalties, but what about when Bayern took theirs? And how did he feel? What was going through his mind?)

Eden takes a terrible penalty.
The keeper saves.
The ball bounces up.
Eden heads the rebound.
The ball bounces into the net.
And now you're gonna believe us!

In 1983/84 I was eight years old and not at the match versus Pompey when One Kerry Dixon missed two penalties. So, I asked a couple of the older codgers on the *Rivals Football* message board of their memories.

RIAZORBLUES writes: "We went on a bad run of missing penalties, so at a League cup game where we were beating City comprehensively, we were awarded a penalty and the whole crowd started chanting for

Pat. He went up and took one of the worst penalties I had ever seen. Sometimes we say things like *"I could have saved that"* and it isn't true, but I genuinely believe I could have saved that one. It got so bad with the pens that the crowd started chanting for Niedzwiecki to take one as he could kick the ball for miles so the reasoning went that he would just blast one in. He never did in a match but they said in one of the programmes that season that he had taken one in training and missed as well!!!"

OSGOODWASGOOD writes: "Kerry's second penalty rebounded off the crossbar. Dixon then missed one in the next game versus Brighton, so Tony MacAndrew took over, then Spackman, followed by Nevin. Eventually Graham Roberts took over when he joined us for the 88/89 season. Incidentally, signing Roberts was the one good thing Campbell did for the club, as Roberts seemed to help calm the squad down. He was obviously a really big influence in us winning promotion. For the record, he scored two last minute penalties, one against Leicester, the other against West Brom. The strange thing was, even though we were Chelsea, when we got a pen that season, we just knew it was going to be a goal. The celebrations of winning those two penalties, in particular, was that the penalty award was celebrated more than the goal that was scored. Sadly, for the team, Roberts nearly got crippled by Perry

Groves, and spent some time out, never to regain his form, and what pace he had, was lost. Roberts ended with a record of 12 out of 12 from the spot. As we all know, Kerry ended on 193 Chelsea goals, shame he was poor from the spot. Portsmouth brought a really good following with them that day. Needless to say, there was trouble outside and on the Underground. It was particularly tasty at Victoria."

OSGOODWASGOOD then went on to explain further about the 83/84 season. He writes: "If there was one season that I could go back and relive, it would be the 83/84 season. From the first game of the season, a 5-0 win at home to Derby and the first away league game, a 2-1 win at Brighton, which followed a 2-1 win at Gillingham in the League Cup, this season will always be my favourite. Friday afternoon in Brighton to find a £10 a night B&B was followed by hours into the night of drinking until the police foolishly ordered us out of the pub and onto the streets. Queue mass punch-ups and running battles, six stabbings and the wrecking of The Pink Coconut. (Followed by the Chelsea fans climbing to the top of the floodlight pylon followed very gingerly half way up by a policeman.) The masses of Chelsea fans that travelled to every away game meant that this season had the lot. It included one of Chelsea's greatest ever games, a 5-3 win at Fulham. The Dixon, Speedie and Nevin front three, arguably the greatest front three in Chelsea's history.

The 3-1 Tuesday night win at Swansea, a great day beside the sea which was followed by what I consider to be the largest 'firm' of travelling supporters to Leeds the following Saturday and a 1-1 draw. From the train going there, to being petrol bombed just outside Leeds, to the escort through the park, (which the police escorting decided to go back to meet the next train load of Chelsea), turned out to be a big mistake. We took over the whole side of their ground with numbers estimated in the papers the following day at 8,000. The Chelsea Invasion left the ground intent on giving Leeds a large dose of GBH and needless to say it was going off all over the place. Cambridge Utd away and they very intelligently gave half the ground to us. Large scale disorder outside before and after the game which we won 1-0. Then up to Geordie Land and the massive blue army turned out again for a table topper which ended 1-1, another following of over 5,000 filled the away end and with Chelsea in their main stand a large amount of UB40 forms descended from the skies. Unfortunately the very good looking pair of girls in the small tea-bar had to make their escape as it was set alight as the masses left their mark....

....Then the mother of all away games, Cardiff, where the Chelsea support took over three sides of the ground. Three really was the magic number that day as Chelsea made a great comeback from three down with fifteen or so minutes left. It was however a comeback that many Chelsea fans, me included, missed because of getting out early for the fisticuffs, running battles all around the ground while the cheers of the Chelsea comeback could be heard. I personally thought we had got hammered but found out over an hour later when getting back to the station that we had infact saved the game. I vowed then never to leave a Chelsea game early, and never have. Another massive turnout of over 15,000 Chelsea fans at Selhurst park to see a 1-0 win just about set us up for promotion. I then travelled to Portsmouth on a Tuesday night with yet another massive turnout, Chelsea squeezed into the away end as well as there being Chelsea in both of their stands. The inevitable trouble broke out with seats being ripped up, all due to a 2-0 lead being given away when a win would have clinched promotion. Promotion followed at the next home game, Leeds, 5-0 with plenty of pitch invasions and the scoreboard being smashed up by the Leeds fans. Loads of trouble on the underground before and during the game led to hundreds of Leeds fans turning up when they were 3-0 down.

Man City away on the Friday night, on TV, saw yet another massive turnout and we easily had a third of the crowd there that night where there were about

22,000 in the ground. A great performance saw us win 2-0 and also included a couple of pitch invasions from Chelsea fans in the City stand. That was followed by the final home game a 3-1 win over Barnsley with more pitch invasions before on to Grimsby for the game that would clinch the Div Two title. A train journey up to Cleethorpes followed by a leisurely walk to the ground and thousands of Chelsea trying to get into the small away end. Me and my mates had tickets but it just didn't matter, fans were just giving the turnstyle operator, I think they only had one gate open, a fiver and he was letting them in, even though all tickets had been bought that away end must of had double the amount in there. Kerry Dixon duly headed the winner and Pat Nevin missed a penalty, that sounds familiar. But what a great day and an absolutely fantastic season to have followed Chelsea in every game. Sadly that will never be repeated and many younger fans will never have had that experience and will never know what it was like to follow our great club back then.

And something else that made that season so special was the first game of the following season and being in amongst 20,000 plus Chelsea fans at Arsenal, the five year wait was complete. The low point of that season was a 3-2 win at Huddersfield, because I had my first ever taste of Gravy on Chips, revolting. I didn't ask for any gravy, the chippy just ladled the stuff on. Couldn't even see the little fuckers. Absolutely no point bothering with the Salt n' Vinegar. Got gravy stains all down me fucking new Fila zipped top."

reference books and essential reading

CELERY! Representing Chelsea in the 1980s

Kelvin Barker

Chelsea Here Chelsea There

Kelvin Barker, David Johnstone and Mark Worrall

At full-time, Eden Hazard's header from his missed penalty wins Chelsea the game against Palace and we are Champions. I take my time leaving Stamford Bridge. I bump into Wickham and we walk up the Fulham Road. Everyone is jubilant – though for me it's not at the level we felt after beating United, then the point at Arsenal and then the win at Leicester – that was like the chase before the pull – and the place is buzzing but I feel more melancholy, I don't know why, but I don't contest it, I just go with it, I reckon that deep down it's because we've done it, plus I won't be here again for possibly four long months.

The Old Bill have already made a horse-shoe shape surrounding a group boozing and celebrating outside Brogans. They won't mess about in an hours time. Bank Holiday Monday tomorrow (I'm working) and they'll clear the streets as quick as they can. Wickham and I continue on. Out the other end of Seagrave Road the Lillie is packed outside and the likewise the Prince of Wales opposite. We turn right onto North End Road and go past the cemetery and then right into Finborough Road. The place, outside and inside, is rammed.

Chidge is the first person I embrace. Smiffy and Chris are with Caz. The bar is deep, too deep, so I get a few cans from the offy next door. Everyone is getting hammered. The names are too many to mention, but we're all here. This is brilliant. I'm aware that I'm working in the morning. Marmite Pete is dancing in the road. I can see a number 74 coming along, I go and pull him out the line of traffic before the bus runs him over.

I stand in the road with the Sherman Chef to try and shepherd supporters back towards the pavement. I can't imagine it will be long until the Old Bill arrive. I push that thought out my head, can in hand, mates on the pavement, mates inside the boozer. The alcohol is taking it's toll, my brain going fuzzy, my mind ticking over, I think about how it feels when I hit a hand in poker on the river. A think of a lyric from *Brand New Start* by Paul Weller about getting myself straight. I look at the ring on my finger and think about the Doris, and the sparkle in her eye when she's sipping wine and finds something funny. I picture a camp fire when it first really catches and the twigs crack and smoke. I look up at Smiffy and think about our trip to Soard. Tying the laces up on a kid who hasn't worn trainers before. I look now at Big Chris and think about Cech saving Arjen Robben's peno in Munich. I look at Drewsy and his pals and I think about them laughing at a joke on the Berk Bus, a green bottle of lager in their hands.

I tell myself I should go home soon – later I'll be pulling the duvet up to my sleeping sons chin and kiss him on the forehead good night. The morning after when I've been at a game, my daughter hugs me and wants to know who scored and what happened. In a month I'll be gagging for the season to start. There'll be a bounce in my step when I'm on the Fulham Road. Hugging my friends at the stall. Seeing Champagne Les raise his Guinness and clink it against mine. Tax Dodger Tommy with his grey satchel over his shoulder and grey Converse on his feet. Vastly Intelligent Keef demanding he buys me a pint. Seeing Famous on his way to the tube to go home and then doing an about turn to accompany me to the boozer. Terri having a pop at me for smoking still. The BFG asking me if everything is all right. Getting a Sambucca in for Cathy. Phil the Butler lifting me up in the air and shouting *hello mate* in my ear. Tall Paul giving me a wink and waiting for the right moment to sing about Molly. Denis telling me about AC Milan at home (again) in February 1966. Jervos lad Zac in awe when I tell him he's going on the pitch pre-match. A geezer in black full of the spirit of justice giving in the fucking big one to those slags at FIFA. Hurry Up Dave giving Jack some fanzines to sell in the boozer at Southampton. Sitting on a train at a station waiting for it take me home. Walking into my local having one for the road and Chelsea Alan singing *We're Top of the League* when he sees me walk in. Putting my head on the pillow, the Doris sleeping next to me, working out how long it is until my next game – sometimes it is ten days, sometime it is forty. We are the Chelsea and we are the best. Waiting for the fixture list. Craving a European Away. Counting down the days. Getting frustrated when TV schedules shift our kick off's. Getting lucky and going to And Leicester. Overtime at work for the football kitty. You work you get paid. You get paid you go to football. Laugh at a sticker on an away pub toilet, or upside down on the back of Old Bill. Chelsea Football Club, I am Stuck on You.

EPILOGUE

Chant of the Season:

In the summer of 2014, there was a push on social media to re-introduce a classic chant which, over the last fifteen, maybe even twenty years, had died out. During Burnley away (our first match of the season) it was brilliant to hear it belted out by the away supporters in the David Fishwick stand: *Ole Ole Ole Ole Chelsea! Chelsea!* The chant quickly picked up pace and became a regular song throughout the season. A special mention goes to the fans of **Chelsea India** who have their own version of the 'Brendan Rogers' song, which goes: *'Breeeeendan. Rooooodgers. Brendan Rogers Liverpool can suck my cock to glory, Demba Ba he scored a goal, you'll tell your kids the story.'* Quite brilliant.

2015 Summer Signing:
Once the season was over, I conducted my own poll, asking fans the question: *If Chelsea could only sign ONE player this summer, who would it be?* The top three results:

Gareth Bale
Cristiano Ronaldo
Sergio Aguero

It was interesting to note that Paul Pobga pulled the same amount of votes as Winston Bogarde and David Mitchell.

2015/2016 Fixture List:
The fixture list was announced only a few days ago. As I write, I've just been working out away games with Big Chris and Smiffy, hoping of course – as all match-going supporters do – that SKY and BT aren't going to mess us around too much.

Thanks for reading. See you next season. Which reminds me, I'd best get an order in sharpish to @cfcstickers before they sell out again.

@WalterOtton
July 13th 2015.

Also by this Author and available from GATE17:

The Red Hand Gang
SHORTS!
#ROE2RO

Coming soon:
Poppy, a novel

Printed in Great Britain
by Amazon